Coralie Bijasson
Photographs: Jean-Baptiste Pellerin
Styling: Dominique Turbé

My First SEWING MACHINE

30 FUN PROJECTS KIDS WILL LOVE TO MAKE

AGE 7+

SEARCH PRESS

Contents

Before you BEGIN...

YOU NEED

→ A pair of special sewing scissors:

You need to look after them carefully and only use them for cutting fabric. If you use sewing scissors to cut paper, they will no longer cut fabric.

→ A pair of scissors for cutting paper

→ A box of pins (use a magnet to keep your pins together)

→ A ruler

→ A pencil

→ A heat-erasable pen

→ Some thread to match your fabric

CHOOSING YOUR FABRIC

For all the projects in this book, we recommend using cotton, as it's an easy fabric to work with and to wash. If you choose a laminated cotton, you have the advantage that it will not fray, but the downside is that the fabric will not glide under your sewing machine foot as easily. For bags and pencil cases, cotton or gabardine fabric is the simplest to handle. Fabrics that work upside down mean that both sides of your bag will look great. For clothes, your best option is midweight cotton.

CUTTING OUT THE PATTERN PIECES

Commercial patterns are generally printed on paper with the seam allowances included. Make sure you check what that seam allowance is, as they do vary. Separate each pattern piece before cutting from fabric.

Fold your fabric right sides together, so you can see the wrong side of the fabric.

For the patterns in this book, use a heat-erasable pen (which disappears when you iron it), to trace round the different pieces as shown in the cutting diagram.

Cut your fabric using a pair of scissors that you only use for fabric. Once you have cut out all the pieces, you can start to sew. Initially, to help you, you can use a pencil to draw on the seam allowances and then sew along your lines. The seam allowance in this book is 1cm (½in).

Pin the different pieces of fabric together. Position your pins at right angles to the seam, approximately every 10cm (4in).

Position your fabric under your machine foot and stitch gently along your line.

FIRST STEPS ON THE MACHINE

Your machine has a spool thread and a bobbin thread. The spool thread is the one on top of the machine and is threaded along the top and down through the needle. You may need an adult to help you at first.

The bobbin is inserted in a recess under the needle called the bobbin case. This is the bottom thread. You may also need to ask an adult to help you to wind the bobbin and insert it.

When you operate your machine, with every stitch, the top thread picks up the bobbin thread.

On your machine, there are two main settings: tension and stitch length. The most common stitch length is number 3. The most common tension is also number 3.

On the sewing machine, you will mainly use two stitches: straight stitch, which is marked like this: - - - and zigzag stitch, which is marked like this: WW

When you start a seam, you should trap the threads under the forefinger of your right hand.

You need to backstitch to secure the start and end of your seam. To do this at the start, work three stitches, then press your machine's reverse button and stitch three stitches back. At the end of your seam, hold the reverse button and stitch three stitches back.

Use both hands to guide your fabric. You should not pull on the fabric but just gently guide it. The fabric should glide under your hands, with hardly any effort.

To start with, take a scrap of fabric and practise sewing straight lines by applying gentle pressure on the pedal of your machine. When you can do this with ease, you are ready to get to work on your first projects.

CLIPPING THE CORNERS

When there is a corner, you often need to clip it, which means trimming the seam allowances close to the seam line. Before you turn your fabric the right way out, clip the corner to 2mm (⅛in) from the seam line. This allows you to form the corner nicely when you turn your work the right way out.

TOPSTITCHING

This means sewing a decorative stitch on the right side of the fabric, often 2mm (⅛in) from the edge of your work. This gives the pieces a professional finish and will close up any opening that you have used to turn your work the right way out.

MACHINE FOOT FOR SEWING IN ZIPS

If you are a sewing in a zip, you need to replace the sewing-machine foot with a special zip (zipper) foot, which allows you to sew close to the teeth of the zip.

GATHERING

Set the stitch length on your machine to number 5.

First sew a row of stitches 5mm (¼in) from the edge of the fabric and then a second row 8mm (⅜in) from the edge of the fabric.

Do not backstitch at the start or finish. Remove your fabric from the machine and pull gently on the bobbin thread (the thread on the bottom) until gathers form and the piece is the right size. Distribute the gathers evenly.

ZIGZAG STITCH

Use zigzag stitch (often stitch number 2 on your machine) to finish your seams and prevent the fabric from fraying, or when you are sewing stretchy fabrics as it helps to retain their elasticity.

SMOCKING

Wind a bobbin of elastic thread by hand.

Insert the bobbin in the machine and sew using straight stitch (stitch number 1 on your machine).

Don't forget to backstitch at the start and end of the stitching.

Now you have the key ingredients for success. So have fun and be as creative as you like! Sewing is a game of patience and precision – and if you have those, you can make anything you can dream of.

MY FIRST SEWING MACHINE

MY *Little sewing*
WORKSHOP

PINCUSHION

SEWING CASE

Pincushion

MATERIALS

→ Cotton fabric 10 x 20cm
   (4 x 8in)
→ Stuffing
→ Needle and thread
→ Sewing machine

CUTTING DIAGRAM, SCALE ¼

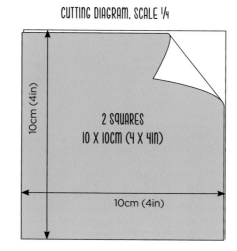

10cm (4in)

2 SQUARES
10 X 10CM (4 X 4IN)

10cm (4in)

METHOD

A CUTTING

1. Cut out two squares, measuring 10 x 10cm (4 x 4in) each.

B SEWING TOGETHER

2. Pin the two squares, right sides together.

3. Sew all round, 1cm (½in) from the edge, leaving a 5cm (2in) opening on one of the sides. You can draw the 1cm (½in) seam allowance on the fabric if it helps, or your sewing machine may have a 1cm (½in) seam allowance marked on the machine in front of the needle.

4. Clip the seam allowances at the corners (see page 9). Turn the cushion the right way out through the opening.

C FINISHING TOUCHES

5. Stuff quite firmly.

6. Sew up the opening by hand. This is usually done with either slipstitch or ladder stitch.

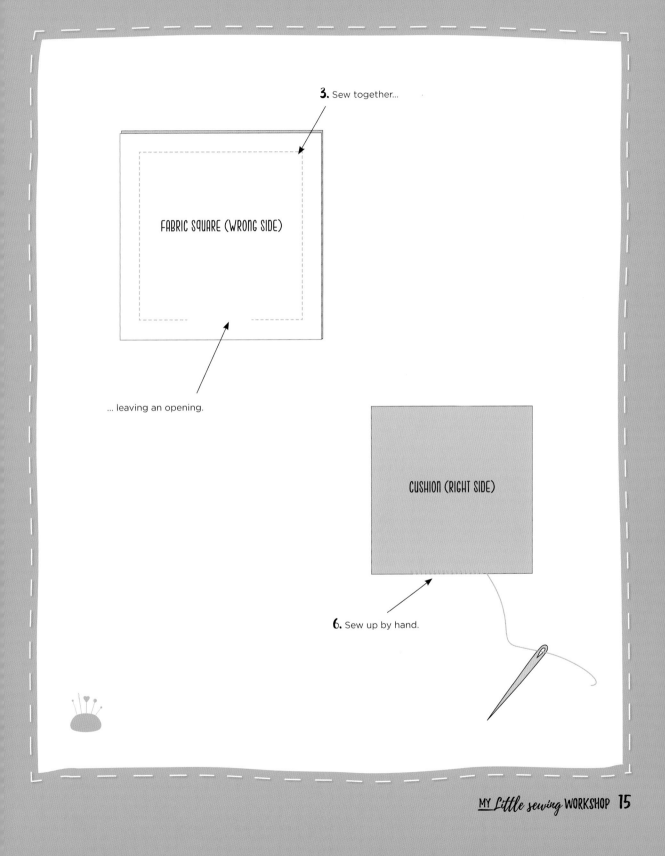

3. Sew together...

FABRIC SQUARE (WRONG SIDE)

... leaving an opening.

CUSHION (RIGHT SIDE)

6. Sew up by hand.

Sewing case

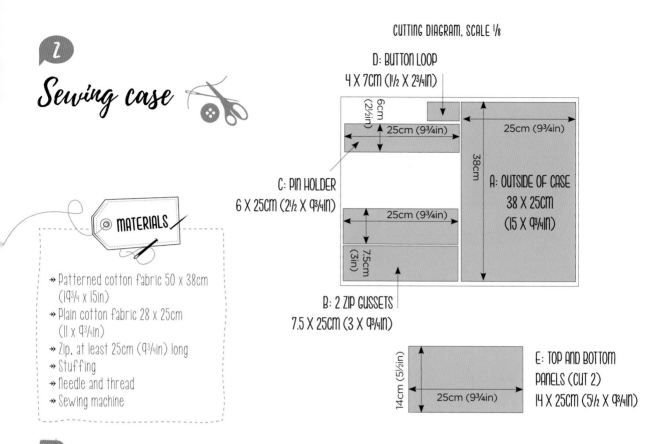

D: BUTTON LOOP
4 X 7CM (1½ X 2¾IN)

6cm (2½in)

25cm (9¾in)

25cm (9¾in)

38cm

C: PIN HOLDER
6 X 25CM (2½ X 9¾IN)

A: OUTSIDE OF CASE
38 X 25CM
(15 X 9¾IN)

25cm (9¾in)

7.5cm (3in)

B: 2 ZIP GUSSETS
7.5 X 25CM (3 X 9¾IN)

14cm (5½in)

25cm (9¾in)

E: TOP AND BOTTOM
PANELS (CUT 2)
14 X 25CM (5½ X 9¾IN)

MATERIALS

→ Patterned cotton fabric 50 x 38cm (19¾ x 15in)
→ Plain cotton fabric 28 x 25cm (11 x 9¾in)
→ Zip, at least 25cm (9¾in) long
→ Stuffing
→ Needle and thread
→ Sewing machine

METHOD

A CUTTING

1. From the patterned cotton fabric cut:
- One rectangle 38 x 25cm (15 x 9¾in) (A)
- Two rectangles 7.5 x 25cm (3 x 9¾in) (B)
- One rectangle 6 x 25cm (2½ x 9¾in) (C)
- One rectangle 4 x 7cm (1½ x 2¾in) (D)

2. From the plain cotton fabric cut:
- Two rectangles 25 x 14cm (9¾ x 5½in) (E)

B PUTTING IN THE ZIP

3. Pin the zip along the edge of one of the zip gussets (piece B), right sides together.

4. Attach the special zip foot to your sewing machine. Adjust the needle position if needed on your machine.

5. Position the foot alongside the teeth of the zip and sew very close to them.

6. Pin and sew the other zip gusset (piece B) to the other side of the zip, right sides together, in the same way.

C ATTACHING THE TOP AND BOTTOM PANELS

7. Reattach the standard foot to the machine. Adjust the needle so that it is central again, if needed.

8. Position one panel right sides together with the free edge of one zip gusset (B). Sew together 1cm (½in) from the edge. Repeat to attach the second piece E to the other zip gusset.

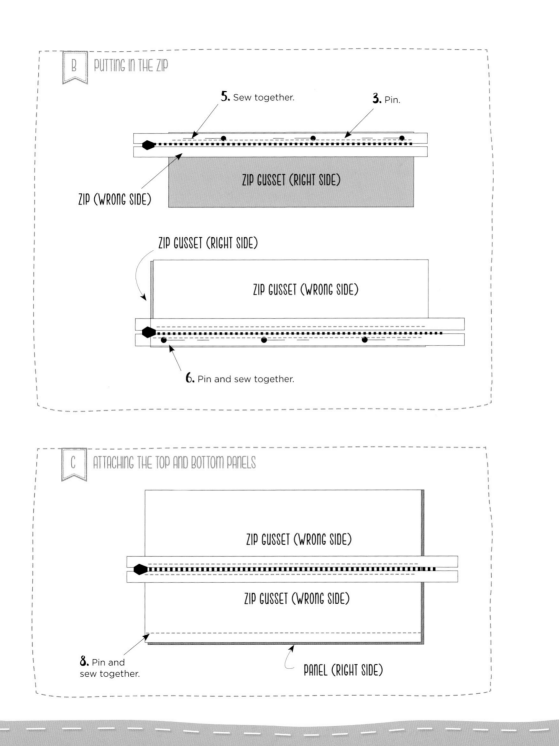

B · PUTTING IN THE ZIP

5. Sew together.

3. Pin.

ZIP (WRONG SIDE)

ZIP GUSSET (RIGHT SIDE)

ZIP GUSSET (RIGHT SIDE)

ZIP GUSSET (WRONG SIDE)

6. Pin and sew together.

C · ATTACHING THE TOP AND BOTTOM PANELS

ZIP GUSSET (WRONG SIDE)

ZIP GUSSET (WRONG SIDE)

8. Pin and sew together.

PANEL (RIGHT SIDE)

Sewing case
(continued)

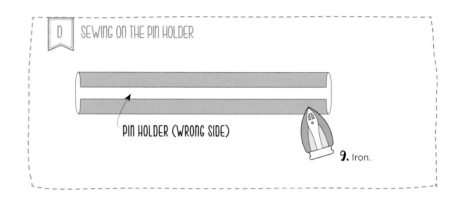

D SEWING ON THE PIN HOLDER

PIN HOLDER (WRONG SIDE)

9. Iron.

🧵 METHOD *(CONTINUED)*

D SEWING ON THE PIN HOLDER

9. Prepare the pin holder by ironing in a 1cm (½in) fold along each long edge of piece C.

10. Lay the wrong side of piece C against the right side of the bottom panel (E), making sure it is roughly centred.

11. Topstitch from one end to the other of piece C, 2mm (⅛in) from the edge on the top and bottom.

12. Slip some stuffing into the pin holder – use a pencil to push the stuffing right inside.

E ATTACHING THE BUTTON LOOP

13. Prepare the button loop (piece D) by ironing in a 1cm (½in) fold along each long edge of the rectangle.

14. Fold it in half lengthways and topstitch, 2mm (⅛in) from the edge.

15. Fold the button loop as shown in the diagram.

16. Sew the button loop to the top of the case on the right side, positioned centrally and within the 1cm (½in) seam allowance.

F SEWING THE CASE TOGETHER

17. Undo the zip by approximately 10cm (4in).

18. Pin the outside (piece A) of the case to the inside, right sides together. Don't worry if they aren't quite the same size. Just use the smaller rectangle as your guide for the seam allowance.

19. Sew right round the case, 1cm (½in) from the edge.

20. Clip the corners (see page 9). Turn the case the right way out through the opening in the zip.

21. Topstitch the top and bottom of the zip-gusset section and right round the whole case.

22. Fold the case into three and sew on the button in the right place for the button loop.

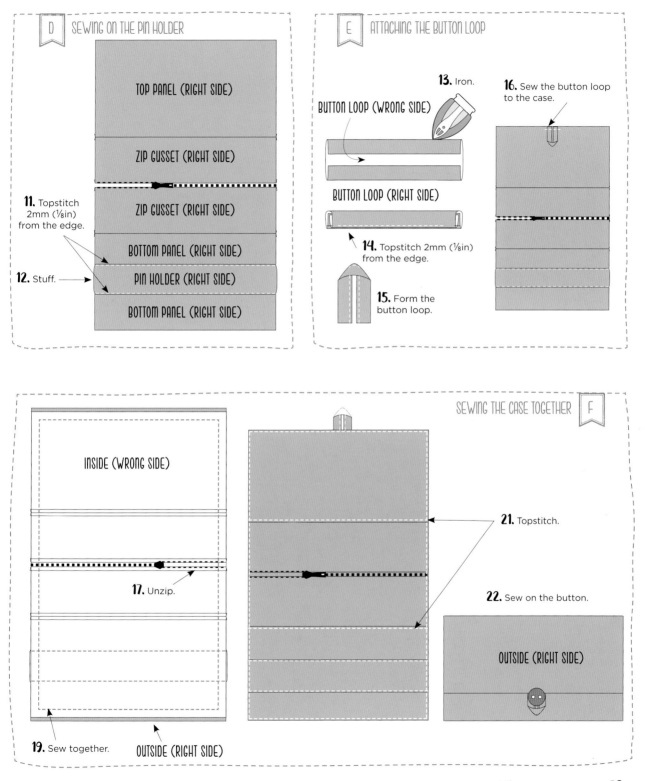

TOP PANEL (RIGHT SIDE)

ZIP GUSSET (RIGHT SIDE)

ZIP GUSSET (RIGHT SIDE)

11. Topstitch 2mm (⅛in) from the edge.

BOTTOM PANEL (RIGHT SIDE)

12. Stuff.

PIN HOLDER (RIGHT SIDE)

BOTTOM PANEL (RIGHT SIDE)

13. Iron.

BUTTON LOOP (WRONG SIDE)

16. Sew the button loop to the case.

BUTTON LOOP (RIGHT SIDE)

14. Topstitch 2mm (⅛in) from the edge.

15. Form the button loop.

INSIDE (WRONG SIDE)

17. Unzip.

21. Topstitch.

22. Sew on the button.

OUTSIDE (RIGHT SIDE)

19. Sew together.

OUTSIDE (RIGHT SIDE)

MY FIRST SEWING MACHINE

FOR ~~my~~ BEDROOM

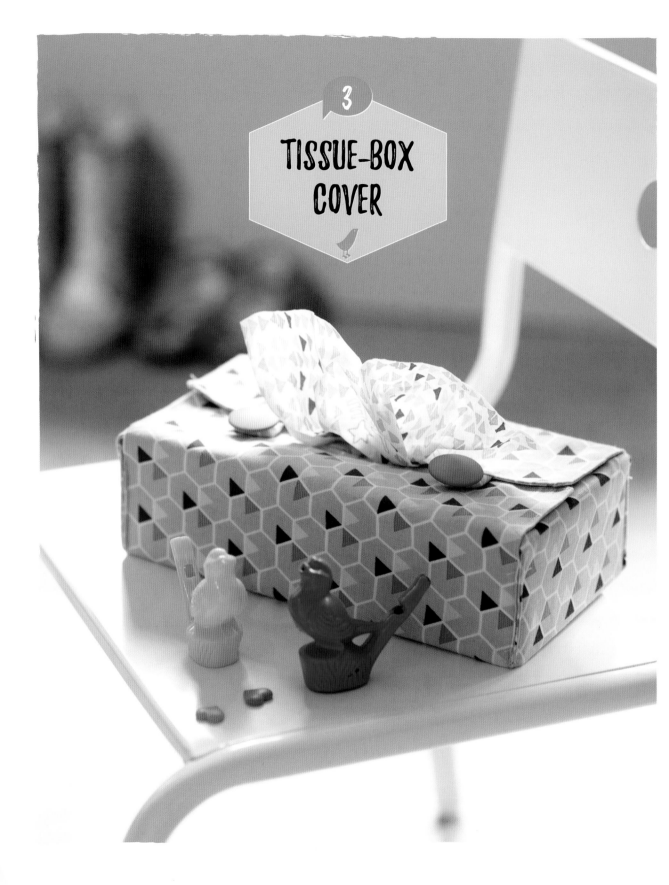

TISSUE-BOX COVER

4

CLOUD CUSHION

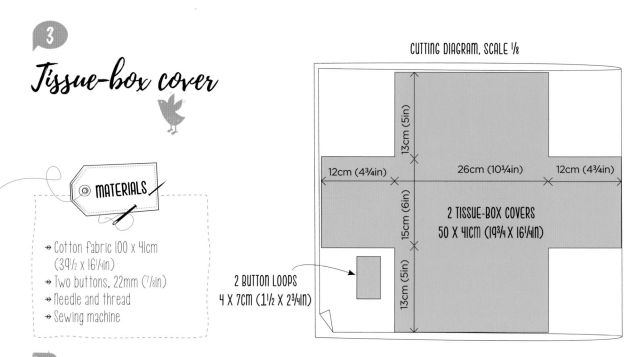

13cm (5in)

12cm (4¾in)   26cm (10¼in)   12cm (4¾in)

15cm (6in)

2 TISSUE-BOX COVERS
50 X 41CM (19¾ X 16¼IN)

13cm (5in)

2 BUTTON LOOPS
4 X 7CM (1½ X 2¾IN)

Tissue-box cover

3

MATERIALS

→ Cotton fabric 100 x 41cm
(39½ x 16¼in)
→ Two buttons, 22mm (⅞in)
→ Needle and thread
→ Sewing machine

METHOD

A CUTTING

1. Fold a 100 x 41cm (39½ x 16¼in) fabric rectangle in half so it's now 50 x 41cm (19¾ x 16¼in). From this, cut out the pieces as shown in the diagram above.

B SEWING ON THE BUTTON LOOPS

2. Iron a 1cm (½in) fold on each long edge of each button loop.

3. Fold each one in half and topstitch, 2mm (⅛in) from the edge.

4. Fold the button loops as shown in the diagram.

5. Sew the button loops to the top of one of the long sides of one of the tissue-box pieces on the right side, 5cm (2in) from the edges. Sew within the 1cm (½in) seam allowance.

C SEWING THE PIECES TOGETHER

6. Lay the two pieces of the tissue-box cover right sides together.

7. Sew right round the edge, taking a 1cm (½in) seam allowance and leaving an opening of approximately 5cm (2in) so that you can turn the cover the right way out.

8. Clip the corners as shown in the diagram.

D COMPLETING THE COVER

9. Turn the box cover the right way out through the opening.

10. Sew up the opening with a few hand stitches – ladder stitch or slipstitch. Alternatively, topstitch all round, 2mm (⅛in) from the edge.

11. Sew the side edges of the box together by hand for approximately 5cm (2in). Again, use ladder stitch or slipstitch.

12. Place a box of tissues inside the box cover and sew on the buttons after aligning them with the button loops.

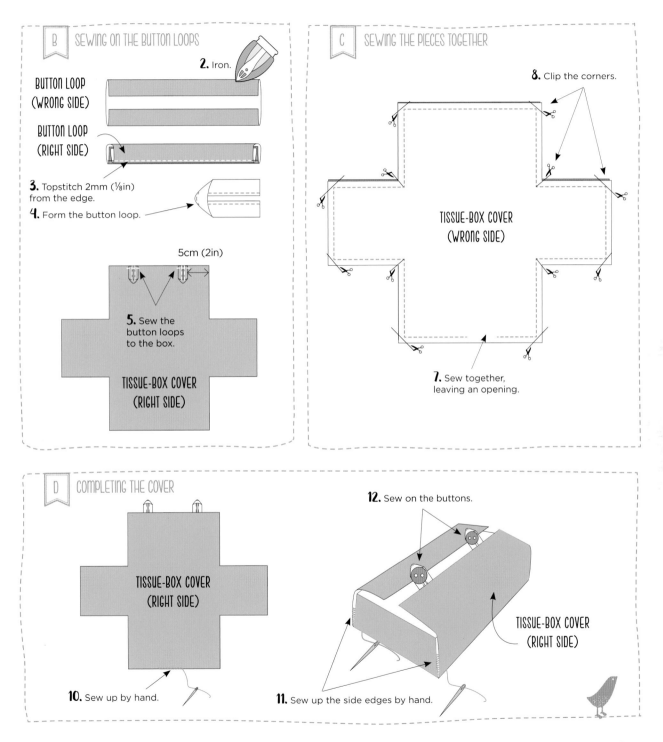

B SEWING ON THE BUTTON LOOPS

2. Iron.

BUTTON LOOP
(WRONG SIDE)

BUTTON LOOP
(RIGHT SIDE)

3. Topstitch 2mm (⅛in)
from the edge.

4. Form the button loop.

5cm (2in)

5. Sew the
button loops
to the box.

TISSUE-BOX COVER
(RIGHT SIDE)

C SEWING THE PIECES TOGETHER

8. Clip the corners.

TISSUE-BOX COVER
(WRONG SIDE)

7. Sew together,
leaving an opening.

D COMPLETING THE COVER

TISSUE-BOX COVER
(RIGHT SIDE)

10. Sew up by hand.

12. Sew on the buttons.

TISSUE-BOX COVER
(RIGHT SIDE)

11. Sew up the side edges by hand.

Cloud cushion

MATERIALS

→ Cotton fabric 104 x 35cm (41 x 13¾in)
→ Stuffing
→ Needle and thread
→ Sewing machine

CUTTING DIAGRAM, SCALE ⅛

35cm (13¾in)

2 CLOUDS
52 X 35cm (20½ X 13¾in)

52cm (20½in)

METHOD

A CUTTING

1. Fold a 104 x 35cm (41 x 13¾in) rectangle of fabric in half so it's now 52 x 35cm (20½ x 13¾in). From this rectangle, cut out two clouds (one through both fabric layers), taking inspiration from the design shown above.

B SEWING TOGETHER

2. Pin the two clouds right sides together.

3. Sew all around, 1cm (½in) from the edge, leaving a 10cm (4in) opening at the base of the cloud.

4. Clip up to the stitching in the angles of the cloud.

5. Turn the cloud the right way out through the gap. If you have a lot of wrinkles in the seam, turn the cushion wrong side out again and clip into the seam allowance where the fabric was wrinkled. Turn right side out again.

C FINISHING TOUCHES

6. Fill with stuffing.

7. Sew up the opening by hand with a few stitches. Use slipstitch or ladder stitch.

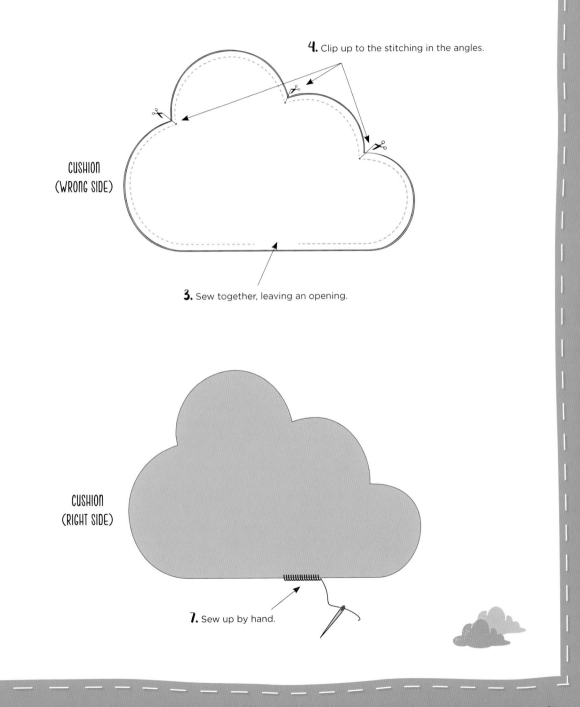

4. Clip up to the stitching in the angles.

CUSHION
(WRONG SIDE)

3. Sew together, leaving an opening.

CUSHION
(RIGHT SIDE)

7. Sew up by hand.

WALL ORGANIZER

6

BASKET TIDY

5

Wall organizer

MATERIALS

→ Cotton fabric 90 x 116cm
  (35½ x 45½in)
→ Needle and thread
→ Sewing machine

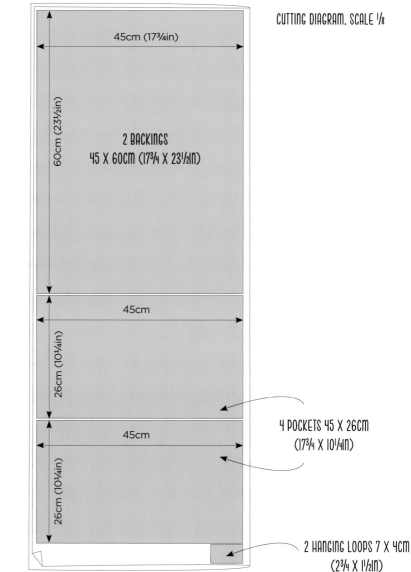

CUTTING DIAGRAM, SCALE ⅛

45cm (17¾in)

60cm (23½in)

2 BACKINGS
45 X 60CM (17¾ X 23½IN)

45cm

26cm (10¼in)

45cm

26cm (10¼in)

4 POCKETS 45 X 26CM
(17¾ X 10¼IN)

2 HANGING LOOPS 7 X 4CM
(2¾ X 1½IN)

METHOD

A CUTTING

1. Fold your fabric in half so it is now 45 x 116cm (17¾ x 45½in) then cut out:
- Two rectangles 45 x 60cm (17¾ x 23½in)
- Four rectangles 45 x 26cm (17¾ x 10¼in)
- Two rectangles 7 x 4cm (2¾ x 1½in)

B ATTACHING THE POCKETS

2. Fold the four 26cm (10¼in) wide rectangles in half, wrong sides together so they are 13 x 45cm (5 x 17¾in).

3. Sew the long edge 0.5cm (¼in) from the edge.

4. On the right side of one of the backing pieces, measuring from the bottom, draw a horizontal line at 13cm (5in), another at 24cm (9½in) and the last one at 35cm (13¾in).

5. Align three of the pockets with the lines. Sew the pockets to the backing, right sides together, 1cm (½in) from the edge.

6. Fold the pockets upwards to hide the seam allowances.

7. Sew the fourth pocket to the bottom of the backing piece, 1cm (½in) from the edge.

8. Topstitch the vertical lines shown in the diagram to divide the pockets.

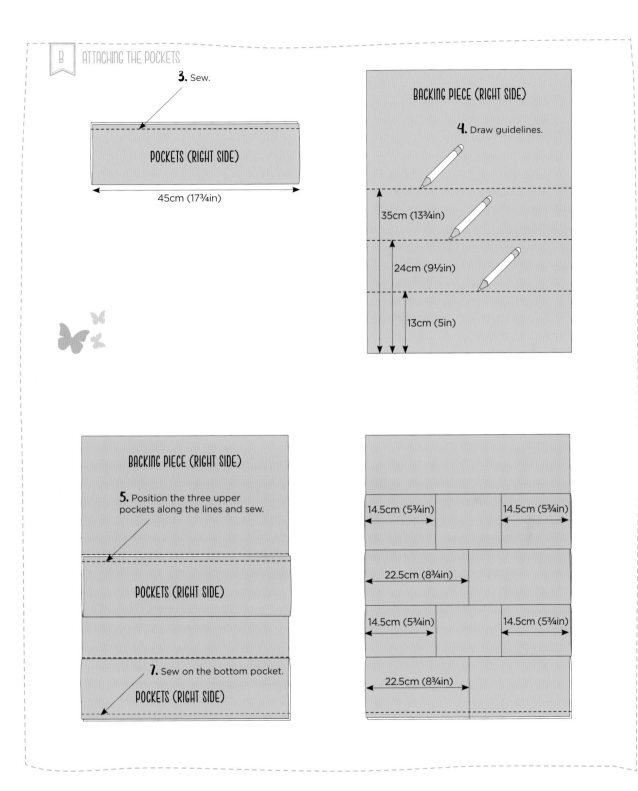

3. Sew.

POCKETS (RIGHT SIDE)

45cm (17¾in)

BACKING PIECE (RIGHT SIDE)

4. Draw guidelines.

35cm (13¾in)

24cm (9½in)

13cm (5in)

BACKING PIECE (RIGHT SIDE)

5. Position the three upper pockets along the lines and sew.

POCKETS (RIGHT SIDE)

7. Sew on the bottom pocket.

POCKETS (RIGHT SIDE)

14.5cm (5¾in)

14.5cm (5¾in)

22.5cm (8¾in)

14.5cm (5¾in)

14.5cm (5¾in)

22.5cm (8¾in)

Wall organizer
(continued)

 **METHOD** *(CONTINUED)*

C ADDING THE HANGING LOOPS

9. Prepare the hanging loops by ironing in a 1cm (½in) fold along each long edge of the two small rectangles.

10. Fold in half and topstitch, 2mm (⅛in) from the edge.

11. Fold the hanging loops as shown in the diagram.

12. Sew the hanging loops to the top of the backing, 8cm (3¼in) from the edges, right sides together. Refer to the diagram for step 5 on page 25 for how to position the loops on the fabric, with the raw edges of the loops on the raw edges of the backing. Sew within the 1cm (½in) seam allowance.

13. Lay the two backing pieces right sides together.

14. Sew right round the organizer, leaving an opening of approximately 8cm (3¼in) so you can turn it the right way out. Clip the corners (see page 9).

15. Turn the right way out and topstitch right round the wall organizer.

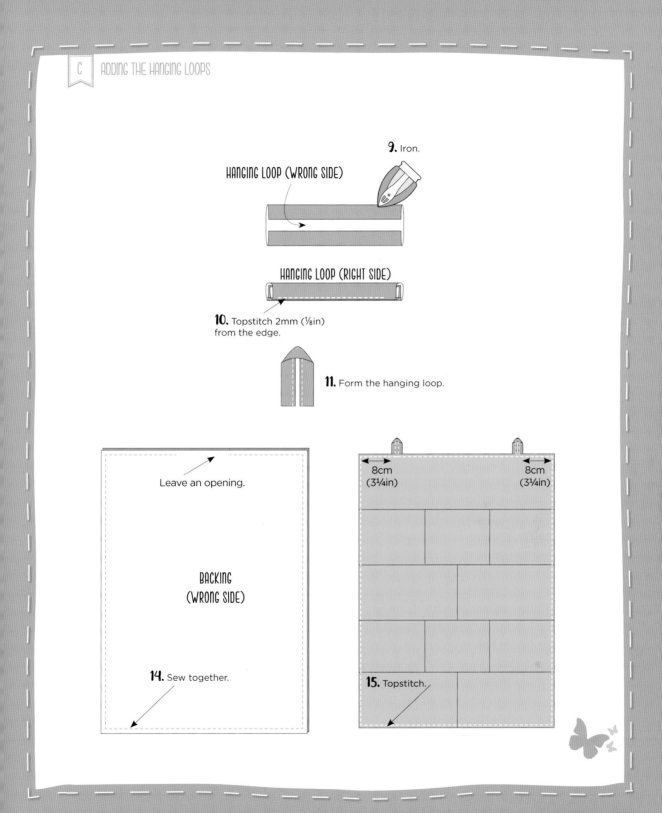

9. Iron.

HANGING LOOP (WRONG SIDE)

HANGING LOOP (RIGHT SIDE)

10. Topstitch 2mm (⅛in) from the edge.

11. Form the hanging loop.

Leave an opening.

BACKING
(WRONG SIDE)

14. Sew together.

8cm
(3¼in)

8cm
(3¼in)

15. Topstitch.

6
Basket tidy

MATERIALS

→ Two squares of fabric 45 x 45cm (18 x 18in): these can be the same fabric or two different ones, as shown on page 29
→ Sewing machine

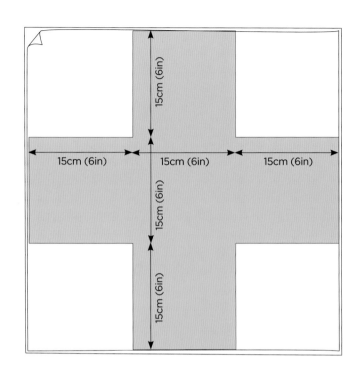

CUTTING DIAGRAM. SCALE ⅙

METHOD

A CUTTING

1. Cut out two crosses, as shown in the diagram above. You can use the squares you cut from the corners to make the keyrings on page 70 if you use ribbon for their hanging loops instead of fabric.

B SEWING TOGETHER

2. Pin and sew adjacent sides of each cross together, right sides facing, 1cm (½in) from the edge. Use the letters on the diagram above right to help.

3. Turn one of the cubes the right way out.

4. Insert one cube in the other so right sides are together.

5. Sew around the top of the cube, leaving an opening of approximately 7cm (2¾in) so you can turn your cube the right way out.

6. Turn the cube the right way out through the opening and topstitch around the top, 2mm (⅛in) from the edge. Fold over the top edge if you wish.

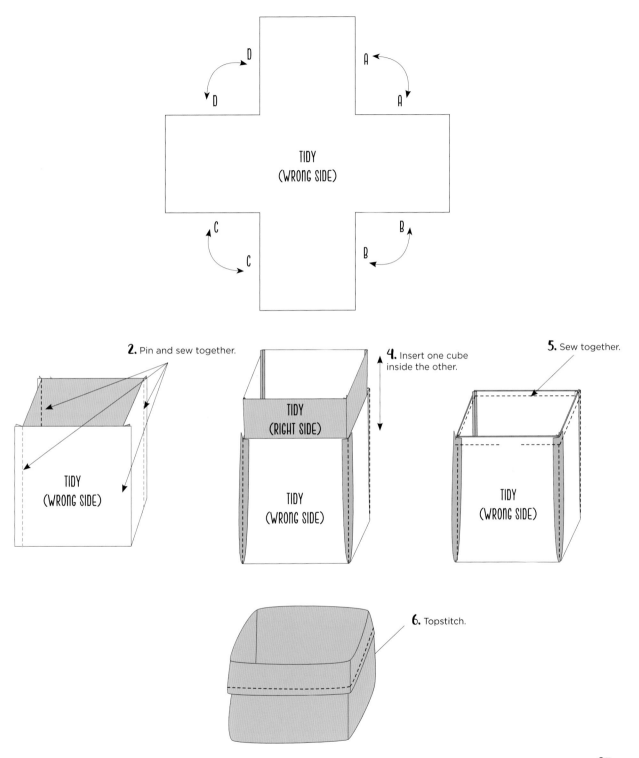

D D

A A

TIDY
(WRONG SIDE)

C C

B B

2. Pin and sew together.

TIDY
(WRONG SIDE)

4. Insert one cube inside the other.

TIDY
(RIGHT SIDE)

TIDY
(WRONG SIDE)

5. Sew together.

TIDY
(WRONG SIDE)

6. Topstitch.

MY FIRST SEWING MACHINE

My BAGS & Accessories

BOWLING BAG

8

PURSE

7

Bowling bag

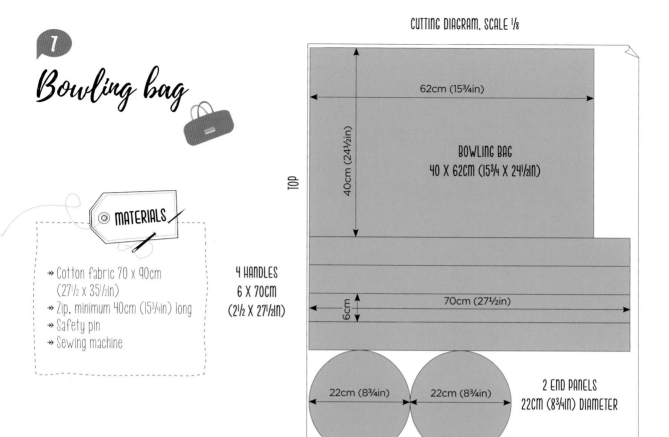

62cm (15¾in)

40cm (24½in)

TOP

BOWLING BAG
40 X 62CM (15¾ X 24½IN)

6cm

70cm (27½in)

4 HANDLES
6 X 70CM
(2½ X 27½IN)

22cm (8¾in)

22cm (8¾in)

2 END PANELS
22CM (8¾IN) DIAMETER

MATERIALS

→ Cotton fabric 70 x 90cm
(27½ x 35½in)
→ Zip, minimum 40cm (15¾in) long
→ Safety pin
→ Sewing machine

METHOD

A CUTTING

1. Cut out:
• One rectangle 40 x 62cm
(15¾ x 24½in)
• Two circles 22cm (8¾in)
diameter
• Four rectangles 6 x 70cm
(2½ x 27½in)

B PUTTING IN THE ZIP

2. Pin the zip along one short
edge of the big rectangle, right
sides together.

3. Attach the special zip foot to
your sewing machine. Adjust the
needle position for use with this
foot, if required.

4. Sew as close to the teeth of
the zip as you can.

5. Pin and sew the other side of
the rectangle to the other side
of the zip, right sides together, in
the same way. Unzip. Cut off any
surplus zip.

C PREPARING THE END PANELS

6. Reattach the standard foot
to the machine and reset the
needle position if required. Sew
a row of gathering stitches
around the edges of the circles.
Make the stitch length as long
as possible and sew 8mm (⅜in)
from the edge just inside the
seam allowance.

7. Remove the fabric from
the machine. Pull gently
on the bobbin thread (the
bottom thread) until the circle
will fit the end of the bag.

8. Distribute the gathers evenly.

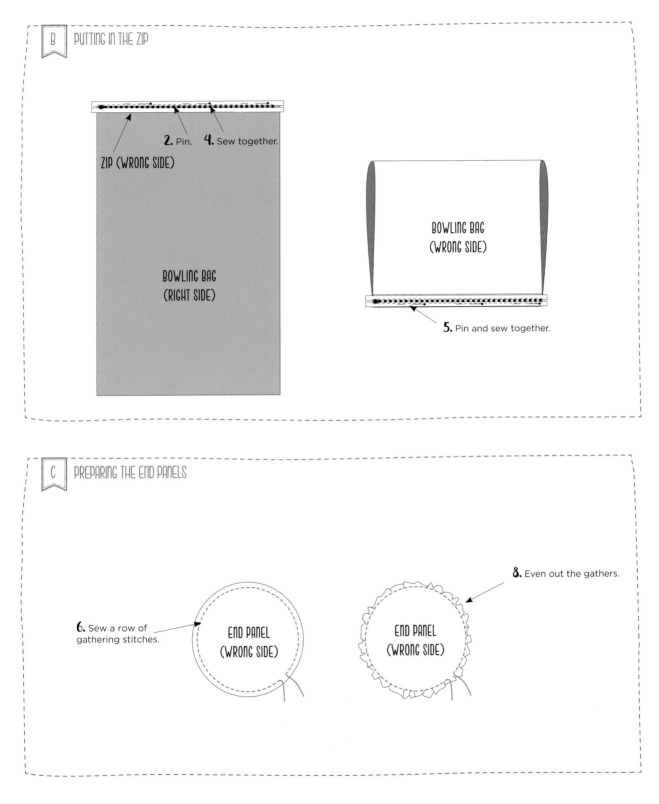

2. Pin. **4.** Sew together.

ZIP (WRONG SIDE)

BOWLING BAG
(RIGHT SIDE)

BOWLING BAG
(WRONG SIDE)

5. Pin and sew together.

C | PREPARING THE END PANELS

8. Even out the gathers.

6. Sew a row of
gathering stitches.

END PANEL
(WRONG SIDE)

END PANEL
(WRONG SIDE)

Bowling bag
(continued)

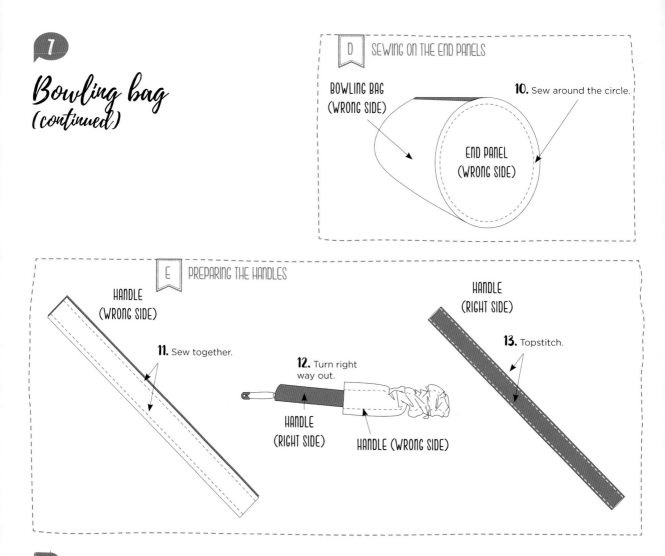

D SEWING ON THE END PANELS

BOWLING BAG
(WRONG SIDE)

10. Sew around the circle.

END PANEL
(WRONG SIDE)

E PREPARING THE HANDLES

HANDLE
(WRONG SIDE)

11. Sew together.

12. Turn right
way out.

HANDLE
(RIGHT SIDE)

HANDLE (WRONG SIDE)

HANDLE
(RIGHT SIDE)

13. Topstitch.

METHOD (CONTINUED)

D   SEWING ON THE END PANELS

9. Leave the zip open.

10. Sew the ends of the bag to the main body of the bag, 1cm (½in) from the edge, right sides together. If you find this difficult, snip partway into the seam allowances at the ends of the main panel at regular intervals – don't go into the stitch line.

E   PREPARING THE HANDLES

11. Take two of the handle pieces and sew the long edges together, right sides facing, 1cm (½in) from the edge. Repeat with the two other handle pieces.

12. Turn the handles the right way out, using a safety pin to help.

13. Topstitch the long sides, 2mm (⅛in) from the edge.

F   SEWING ON THE HANDLES

14. Position the handles 8cm (3¼in) from the ends of the bag and 12cm (4¾in) from the zip.

15. Fold under 1cm (½in) at each end then pin and sew to the bag, forming a cross shape as shown in the diagram.

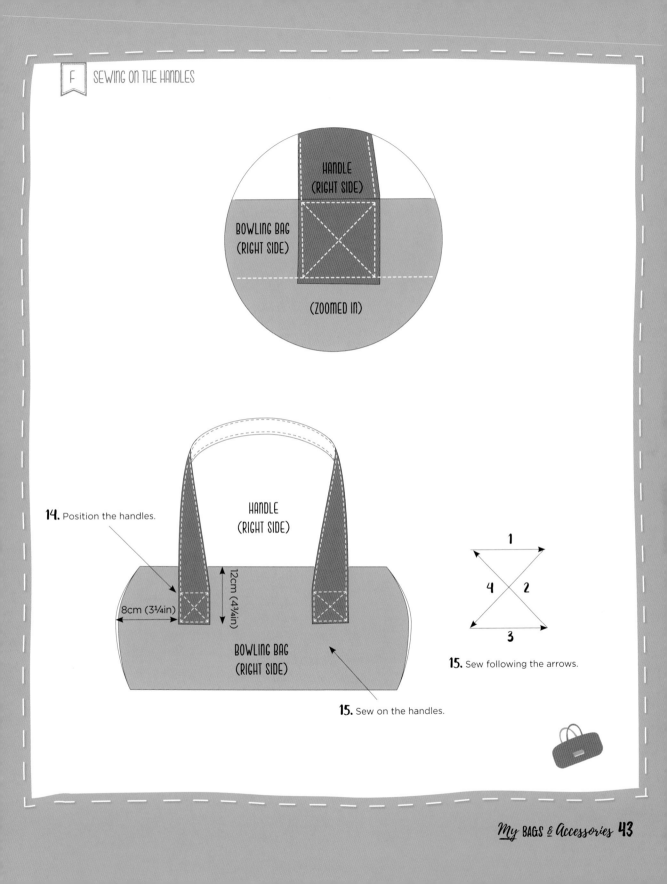

HANDLE
(RIGHT SIDE)

BOWLING BAG
(RIGHT SIDE)

(ZOOMED IN)

14. Position the handles.

HANDLE
(RIGHT SIDE)

12cm (4¾in)

8cm (3¼in)

BOWLING BAG
(RIGHT SIDE)

15. Sew on the handles.

1

4   2

3

15. Sew following the arrows.

8

Purse

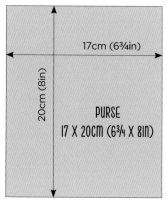

CUTTING DIAGRAM, SCALE ⅛

17cm (6¾in)

20cm (8in)

PURSE
17 X 20CM (6¾ X 8IN)

⊚ MATERIALS

→ Laminated or standard cotton fabric 20 x 17cm (8 x 6¾in)
→ Zip, minimum 17cm (6¾in) long
→ Sewing machine

METHOD

A CUTTING

1. Cut a rectangle 20 x 17cm (8 x 6¾in) from the cotton if you haven't already done so.

B PUTTING IN THE ZIP

2. Pin the zip along one 17cm (6¾in) edge, right sides together.

3. Attach the special zip foot on your sewing machine and adjust the needle position if required for your machine.

4. Sew as close to the teeth of the zip as you can.

5. In the same way, pin and sew the other short edge of the rectangle to the other side of the zip, right sides together.

C SEWING UP THE SIDES OF THE PURSE

6. Unzip halfway.

7. With right sides together, arrange the purse so the zip is approximately 3cm (1¼in) from the top of the rectangle.

8. Reattach the standard foot to the machine and readjust the needle position if required. Sew up the sides of the purse, 1cm (½in) from the edge.

9. Cut off any surplus zip.

10. Turn the purse the right way out through the opening in the zip.

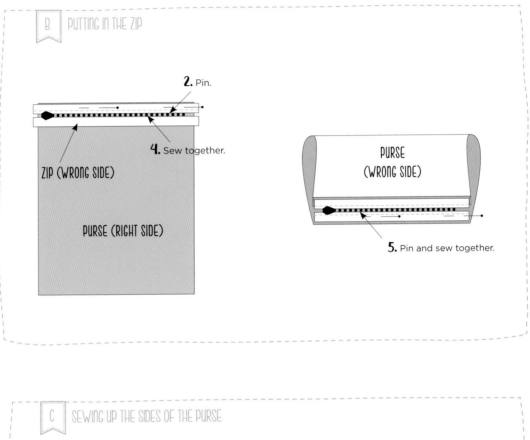

2. Pin.

4. Sew together.

ZIP (WRONG SIDE)

PURSE (RIGHT SIDE)

PURSE
(WRONG SIDE)

5. Pin and sew together.

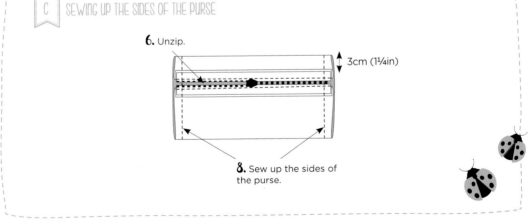

6. Unzip.

3cm (1¼in)

8. Sew up the sides of the purse.

9

PRINCESS TOTE BAG

10

BACKPACK

Princess tote bag

MATERIALS

→ Cotton fabric 64 x 77cm (25¾ x 30¼in)
→ Safety pin
→ Sewing machine

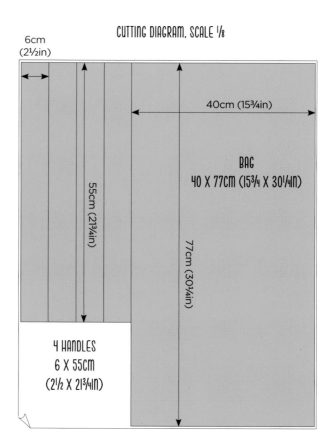

CUTTING DIAGRAM, SCALE ⅛

6cm (2½in)

40cm (15¾in)

55cm (21¾in)

BAG
40 X 77CM (15¾ X 30¼in)

77cm (30¼in)

4 HANDLES
6 X 55CM
(2½ X 21¾in)

METHOD

A CUTTING

1. Cut out:
- One rectangle of cotton fabric 40 x 77cm (15¾ x 30¼in)
- Four rectangles 6 x 55cm (2½ x 21¾in)

B SEWING THE BAG

2. Fold the large rectangle in half, bringing the short sides right sides together, and sew up the sides of the bag, 1cm (½in) from the edge.

3. Form the hems at the top of the bag by folding over 1cm (½in) then 4cm (1½in).

4. Topstitch 2mm (⅛in) from the edge of the hem.

5. Draw a 9 x 9cm (3½ x 3½in) square at each bottom corner on the front and back of the bag.

6. Open out the corners to make 'box corners' by pushing the sewn edge down against the bottom fold so it makes a point. Follow the arrow in the diagram.

7. Sew along the drawn line.

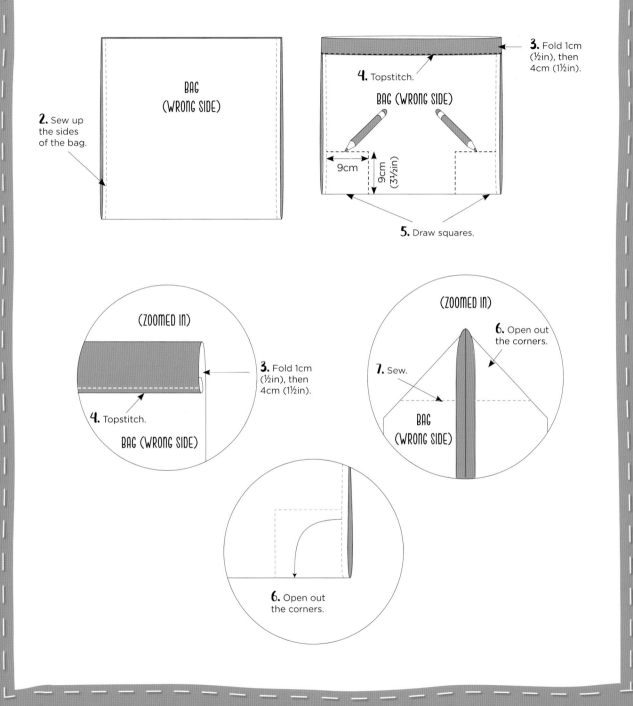

BAG
(WRONG SIDE)

2. Sew up the sides of the bag.

3. Fold 1cm (½in), then 4cm (1½in).

4. Topstitch.

BAG (WRONG SIDE)

9cm

9cm
(3½in)

5. Draw squares.

(ZOOMED IN)

3. Fold 1cm (½in), then 4cm (1½in).

4. Topstitch.

BAG (WRONG SIDE)

(ZOOMED IN)

6. Open out the corners.

7. Sew.

BAG
(WRONG SIDE)

6. Open out the corners.

Princess tote bag
(continued)

![sewing machine icon] **METHOD** *(CONTINUED)*

C PREPARING THE HANDLES

8. Take two of the handle rectangles and sew the long edges together, right sides facing, 1cm (½in) from the edge. Repeat with the two other handle pieces.

9. Turn the handles the right way out, using a safety pin to help.

10. Topstitch the long sides, 2mm (⅛in) from the edge.

D SEWING ON THE HANDLES

11. Turn the bag the right way out. Position the handles 8cm (3¼in) from the edges of the bag.

12. Fold under 1cm (½in) at each end then pin and sew to the bag, forming a cross shape as shown in the diagram.

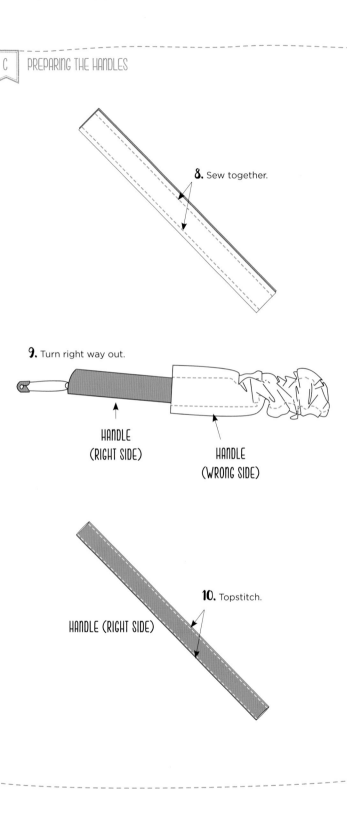

C PREPARING THE HANDLES

8. Sew together.

9. Turn right way out.

HANDLE
(RIGHT SIDE)

HANDLE
(WRONG SIDE)

10. Topstitch.

HANDLE (RIGHT SIDE)

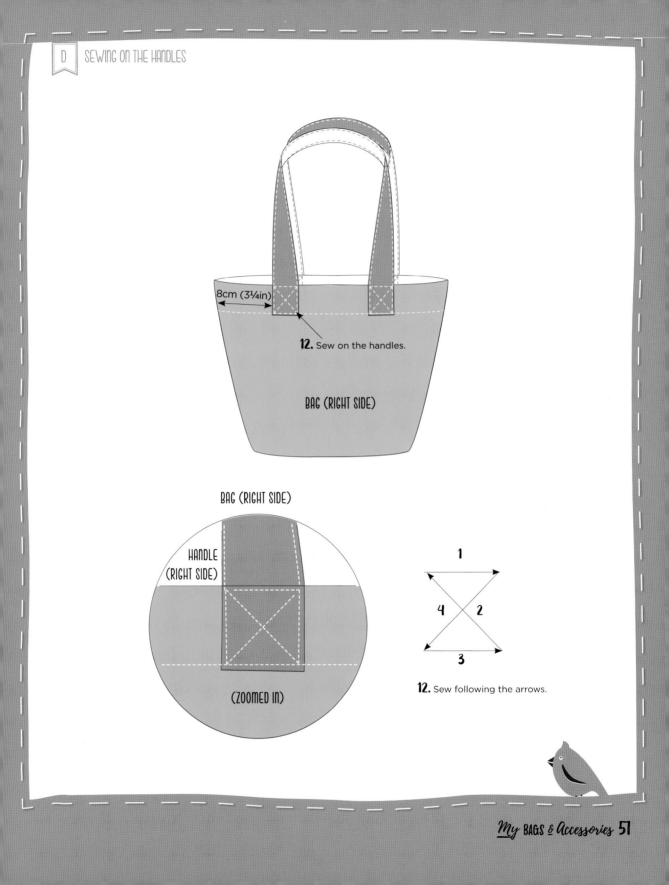

8cm (3¼in)

12. Sew on the handles.

BAG (RIGHT SIDE)

BAG (RIGHT SIDE)

HANDLE
(RIGHT SIDE)

(ZOOMED IN)

1

4   2

3

12. Sew following the arrows.

10

Backpack

MATERIALS

→ Fabric 60 x 95cm (23¾ x 37½in)
→ Elastic, 1cm (½in) wide and 40cm (15¾in) long
→ Button, 22mm (⅞in)
→ Safety pin
→ Sewing machine

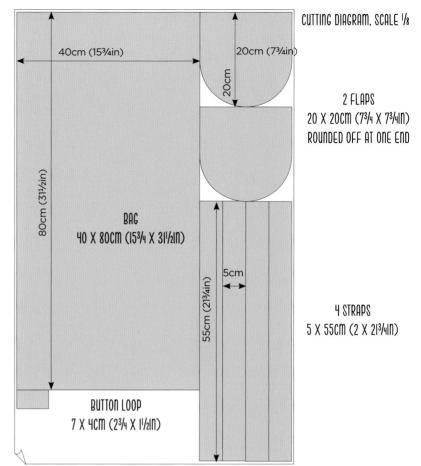

CUTTING DIAGRAM, SCALE ⅛

40cm (15¾in)

20cm (7¾in)

20cm

2 FLAPS
20 X 20CM (7¾ X 7¾IN)
ROUNDED OFF AT ONE END

80cm (31½in)

BAG
40 X 80CM (15¾ X 31½IN)

55cm (21¾in)

5cm

4 STRAPS
5 X 55CM (2 X 21¾IN)

BUTTON LOOP
7 X 4CM (2¾ X 1½IN)

METHOD

A CUTTING

1. Cut out:
- One rectangle 40 x 80cm (15¾ x 31½in)
- Four rectangles 5 x 55cm (2 x 21¾in)
- One rectangle 7 x 4cm (2¾ x 1½in)
- Two squares 20 x 20cm (7¾ x 7¾in), rounded off at one end as shown in the diagram

B PREPARING THE BUTTON LOOP

2. Iron a 1cm (½in) fold along each long edge of the 7 x 4cm (2¾ x 1½in) rectangle.

3. Fold the piece in half and topstitch, 2mm (⅛in) from the edge.

4. Fold the button loop as shown in the diagram.

5. Sew on the button loop, right sides together, in the middle of one of the flaps, within the 1cm (½in) seam allowance.

C SEWING THE FLAP

6. Sew the two flap pieces right sides together, around the curved edge.

7. Turn the flap the right way out.

8. Topstitch around the curve, 2mm (⅛in) from the edge.

D PREPARING THE STRAPS

9. Take two of the strap pieces and sew the long edges together, right sides facing, 1cm (½in) from the edge. Repeat with the other two strap pieces.

10. Turn the straps the right way out, using a safety pin to help.

11. Topstitch the long sides, 2mm (⅛in) from the edge.

E SEWING ON THE STRAPS

12. Position and sew on the straps 35cm (13¾in) from the top of the bag, right sides together.

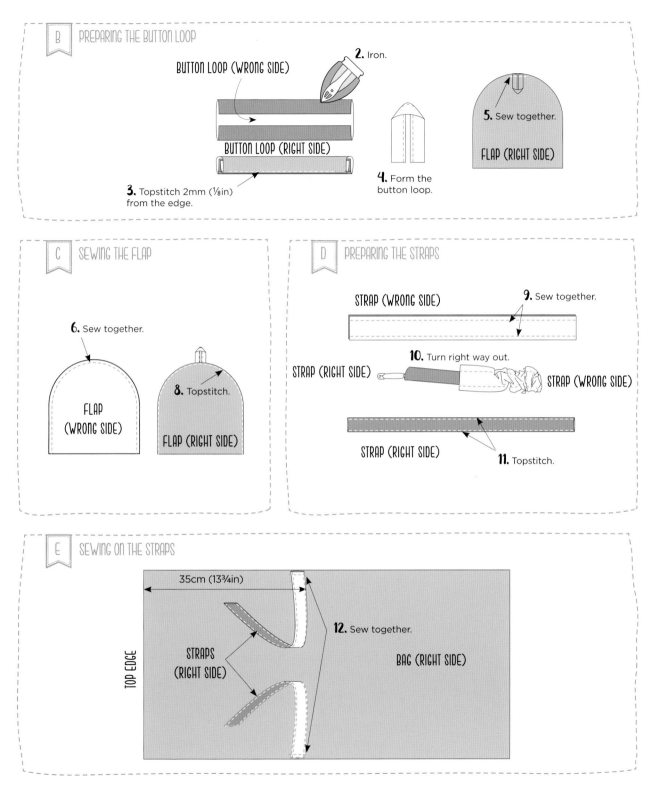

B PREPARING THE BUTTON LOOP

BUTTON LOOP (WRONG SIDE)

2. Iron.

BUTTON LOOP (RIGHT SIDE)

3. Topstitch 2mm (⅛in) from the edge.

4. Form the button loop.

5. Sew together.

FLAP (RIGHT SIDE)

C SEWING THE FLAP

6. Sew together.

FLAP (WRONG SIDE)

8. Topstitch.

FLAP (RIGHT SIDE)

D PREPARING THE STRAPS

STRAP (WRONG SIDE)

9. Sew together.

STRAP (RIGHT SIDE)

10. Turn right way out.

STRAP (WRONG SIDE)

STRAP (RIGHT SIDE)

11. Topstitch.

E SEWING ON THE STRAPS

35cm (13¾in)

TOP EDGE

12. Sew together.

STRAPS (RIGHT SIDE)

BAG (RIGHT SIDE)

Backpack
(continued)

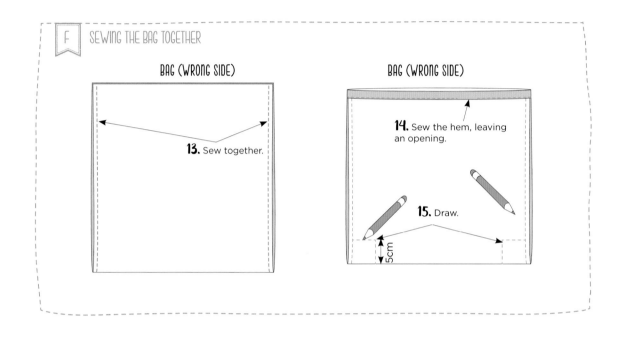

F   SEWING THE BAG TOGETHER

BAG (WRONG SIDE)

13. Sew together.

BAG (WRONG SIDE)

14. Sew the hem, leaving an opening.

15. Draw.

5cm

METHOD (CONTINUED)

F   SEWING THE BAG TOGETHER

13. Fold the bag in half, right sides facing, bringing the two short edges together and sew the sides 1cm (½in) from the edge.

14. Hem at the top of the bag by folding over 1cm (½in), then 2cm (¾in) and topstitching 2mm (⅛in) from the bottom of the hem. Leave a 5cm (2in) opening so you can feed through the elastic.

15. Draw a 5 x 5cm (2 x 2in) square at each bottom corner on the front and back of the bag.

16. Open out the corners to make 'box corners' by pushing the sewn edge down against the bottom fold so it makes a point. Follow the arrow in the diagram.

17. Sew along the drawn line.

18. Turn the bag right side out. Place the flap in the middle of the side that doesn't have the opening for elastic (see step 14).

Position the straps under the flap, tack them in place to stop them sliding out of place as you stitch, then sew through all layers just below the hem.

19. Using a safety pin, thread the elastic through the hem.

20. Sew the ends of the elastic together and sew up the opening in the hem.

21. Sew the button on to the bag after aligning it with the button loop.

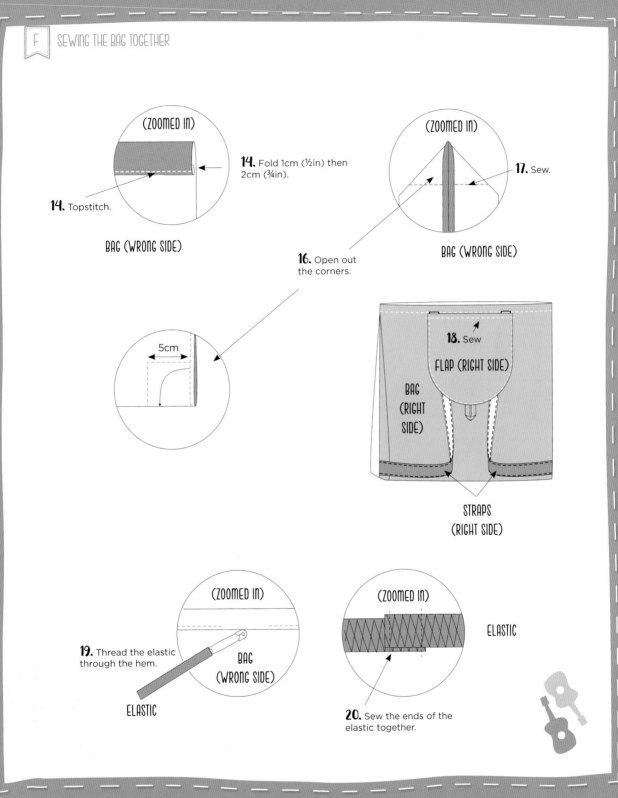

(ZOOMED IN)

14. Fold 1cm (½in) then 2cm (¾in).

14. Topstitch.

BAG (WRONG SIDE)

(ZOOMED IN)

17. Sew.

BAG (WRONG SIDE)

16. Open out the corners.

5cm

18. Sew

FLAP (RIGHT SIDE)

BAG (RIGHT SIDE)

STRAPS (RIGHT SIDE)

(ZOOMED IN)

19. Thread the elastic through the hem.

BAG (WRONG SIDE)

ELASTIC

(ZOOMED IN)

ELASTIC

20. Sew the ends of the elastic together.

11

SHOULDER BAG

12

EARPHONE CASE

Shoulder bag

MATERIALS

→ Cotton fabric 80 x 72cm (31½ x 28¼in)
→ Safety pin
→ Sewing machine

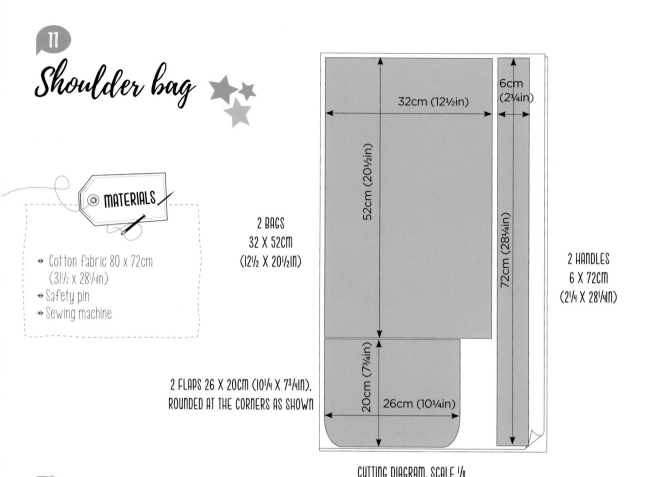

2 BAGS
32 X 52CM
(12½ X 20½IN)

32cm (12½in)

52cm (20½in)

6cm (2¼in)

72cm (28¼in)

2 HANDLES
6 X 72CM
(2¼ X 28¼IN)

20cm (7¾in)

26cm (10¼in)

2 FLAPS 26 X 20CM (10¼ X 7¾IN),
ROUNDED AT THE CORNERS AS SHOWN

CUTTING DIAGRAM, SCALE ⅛

METHOD

A CUTTING

1. Fold the fabric in half so it is 40 x 72cm (15¾ x 28¼in). Cut through both layers to cut out:
• Two rectangles 32 x 52cm (12½ x 20½in)
• Two rectangles with rounded corners 26 x 20cm (10¼ x 7¾in)
• Two rectangles 6 x 72cm (2¼ x 28¼in): for fun, you can use two different fabrics for each one as we did

B PREPARING THE MAIN BODY OF THE BAG

2. Fold one large outer-fabric rectangle, right sides together.

3. Sew up the sides of the bag, 1cm (½in) from the edge.

4. Draw a 3 x 3cm (1¼ x 1¼in) square at each bottom corner on the front and back of the bag.

5. Open out the corners to make 'box corners' by pushing the sewn edge down against the bottom fold so it makes a point. Follow the arrow in the diagram.

6. Sew along the line.

7. Repeat steps 1–6 with the second bag piece.

8. Turn one bag piece (for the outer bag) the right way out. Keep the other bag piece the wrong way out.

C PREPARING THE FLAP

9. Place the two flap pieces right sides together. Sew around the outside, 1cm (½in) from the edge, leaving the straight edge open.

10. Turn the flap the right way out and topstitch 2mm (⅛in) right around the flap to hold the layers together.

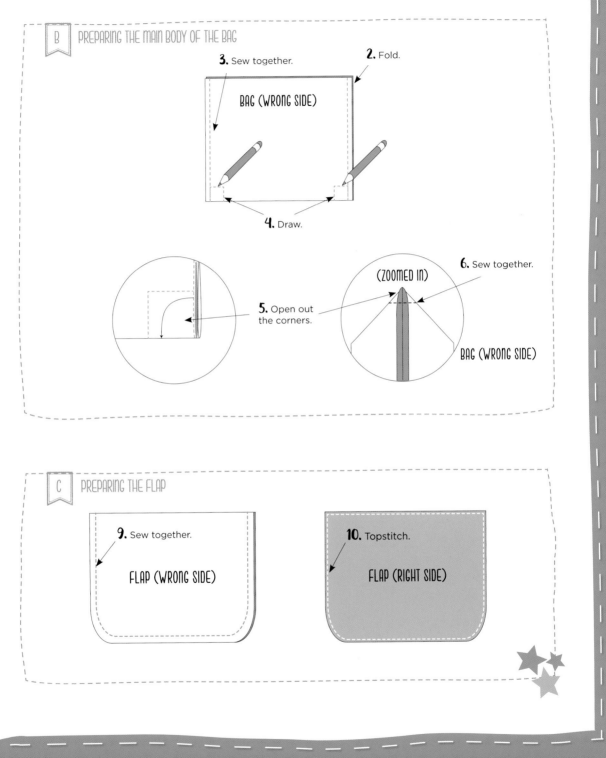

B PREPARING THE MAIN BODY OF THE BAG

3. Sew together.

2. Fold.

BAG (WRONG SIDE)

4. Draw.

5. Open out the corners.

(ZOOMED IN)

6. Sew together.

BAG (WRONG SIDE)

C PREPARING THE FLAP

9. Sew together.

FLAP (WRONG SIDE)

10. Topstitch.

FLAP (RIGHT SIDE)

Shoulder bag
(continued)

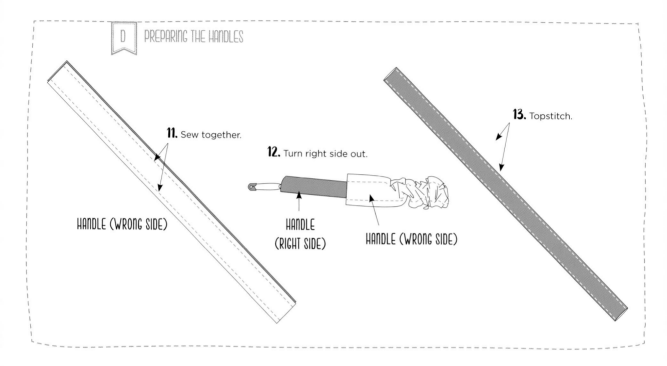

D PREPARING THE HANDLES

11. Sew together.

12. Turn right side out.

13. Topstitch.

HANDLE (WRONG SIDE)

HANDLE
(RIGHT SIDE)

HANDLE (WRONG SIDE)

METHOD

D PREPARING THE HANDLES

11. Pin the two handle pieces right sides together. Sew along both long edges, taking a 1cm (½in) seam allowance.

12. Turn the handle the right way out, using a safety pin to help.

13. Topstitch the long sides, 2mm (⅛in) from the edge.

E SEWING THE BAG TOGETHER

14. Pin the flap to one of the long sides of the outer bag piece and each end of the handle to the short sides. Sew within the 1cm (½in) seam allowance.

15. Slip the outer bag inside the lining, right sides together.

16. Sew round the top, 1cm (½in) from the edge, leaving a 10cm (4in) opening.

17. Turn the bag the right way out through the opening.

F FINISHING TOUCHES

18. Topstitch around the top of the shoulder bag, 2mm (⅛in) from the edge.

19. You can also topstitch along the sides of the shoulder bag, 2mm (⅛in) from the edge.

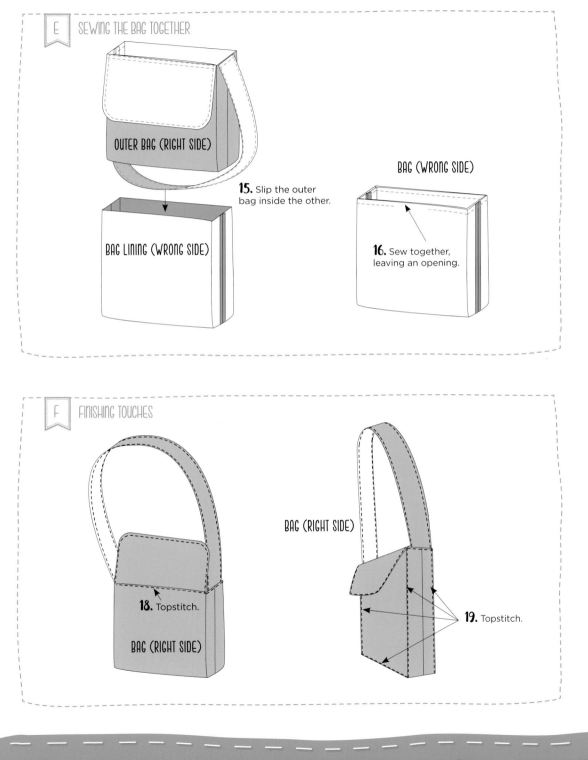

E SEWING THE BAG TOGETHER

OUTER BAG (RIGHT SIDE)

15. Slip the outer bag inside the other.

BAG LINING (WRONG SIDE)

BAG (WRONG SIDE)

16. Sew together, leaving an opening.

F FINISHING TOUCHES

18. Topstitch.

BAG (RIGHT SIDE)

BAG (RIGHT SIDE)

19. Topstitch.

Earphone case

12

MATERIALS

→ Laminated or standard cotton fabric 10 x 25cm (4 x 9¾in)
→ Zip, minimum 10cm (4in) long
→ Sewing machine

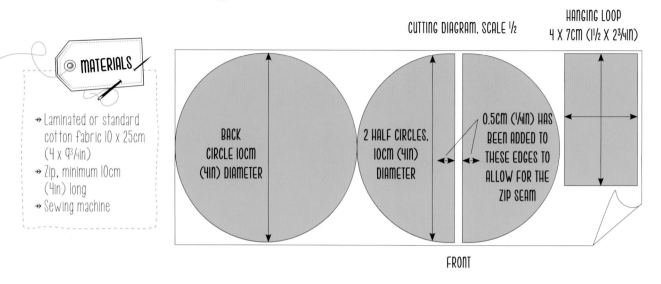

CUTTING DIAGRAM, SCALE ½

HANGING LOOP
4 X 7CM (1½ X 2¾IN)

BACK
CIRCLE 10CM
(4IN) DIAMETER

2 HALF CIRCLES,
10CM (4IN)
DIAMETER

0.5CM (¼IN) HAS
BEEN ADDED TO
THESE EDGES TO
ALLOW FOR THE
ZIP SEAM

FRONT

METHOD

A PREPARATION

1. Photocopy the shapes above at 200%.

2. Cut out the photocopied shapes.

3. Trace the shapes on to the fabric and cut out.

4. Fold and iron a 1cm (½in) fold along each long side of the hanging loop.

5. Fold in half and topstitch, 2mm (⅛in) from the edge.

6. Sew the hanging loop (centred) to one of the front pieces, within the 1cm (½in) seam allowance.

B PUTTING IN THE ZIP

7. Pin the zip right sides together along the straight edge of one of the front pieces, aligning the raw edges.

8. Attach the zip foot to your sewing machine and adjust the needle position if needed.

9. Sew along the right-hand edge of the zip, sewing as close to the teeth of the zip as you can.

10. In the same way, pin and sew the other front piece to the other side of the zip, right sides together.

C SEWING TOGETHER

11. Unzip halfway.

12. Reattach the standard foot to the machine and readjust the needle position. Pin the front and back of the earphone case right sides together and sew all round, 1cm (½in) from the edge. Don't worry if your two pieces are not quite the same size – just stitch in a circle, not going too close to the edge of either piece.

13. Cut off any surplus zip.

14. Turn the earphone case the right way out to finish.

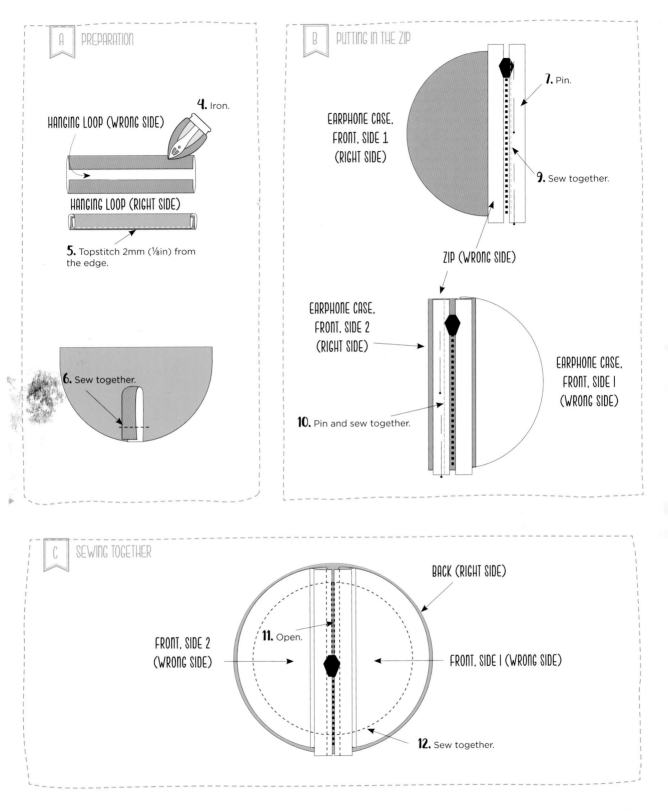

A · PREPARATION

HANGING LOOP (WRONG SIDE)

4. Iron.

HANGING LOOP (RIGHT SIDE)

5. Topstitch 2mm (⅛in) from the edge.

6. Sew together.

B · PUTTING IN THE ZIP

EARPHONE CASE, FRONT, SIDE 1 (RIGHT SIDE)

7. Pin.

9. Sew together.

ZIP (WRONG SIDE)

EARPHONE CASE, FRONT, SIDE 2 (RIGHT SIDE)

EARPHONE CASE, FRONT, SIDE 1 (WRONG SIDE)

10. Pin and sew together.

C · SEWING TOGETHER

BACK (RIGHT SIDE)

FRONT, SIDE 2 (WRONG SIDE)

11. Open.

FRONT, SIDE 1 (WRONG SIDE)

12. Sew together.

SHOPPING BAG

13

KEYRING

Shopping bag

MATERIALS

→ Cotton fabric 59 x 120cm
  (23¼ x 47¼in)
→ Safety pin
→ Sewing machine

CUTTING DIAGRAM. SCALE ⅛

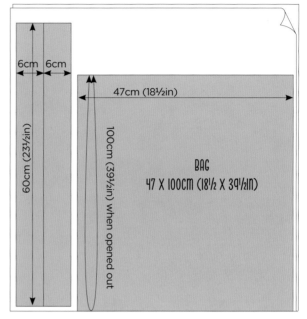

6cm 6cm

60cm (23¾in)

100cm (39½in) when opened out

47cm (18½in)

BAG
47 X 100CM (18½ X 39½IN)

4 HANDLES
6 X 60CM (2¼ X 23½IN)

METHOD

A CUTTING

1. Cut out:
• One rectangle 47 x 100cm
  (18½ x 39½in)
• Four rectangles 6 x 60cm
  (2¼ x 23½in)
To do this, fold the fabric in
half widthwise, cut two straps
through both layers and either
unfold to cut the bag piece
or cut a rectangle 47 x 50cm
(18½ x 19¾in) on the fold.

B PREPARING THE BODY OF THE BAG

2. Fold the bag in half, right sides
together so it is 47 x 50cm (18½
x 19¾in) and sew up the sides,
1cm (½in) from the edge.

3. Form the hems at the top of
the bag by folding over 1cm (½in)
then 4cm (1½in).

4. Topstitch 2mm (⅛in) from the
edge of the hem.

5. Draw a 5 x 5cm (2 x 2in)
square at each bottom corner on
the front and back of the bag.

6. Open out the corners to make
'box corners' by pushing the
sewn edge down against the
bottom fold so it makes a point.
Follow the arrow in the diagram.

7. Sew along the drawn line.

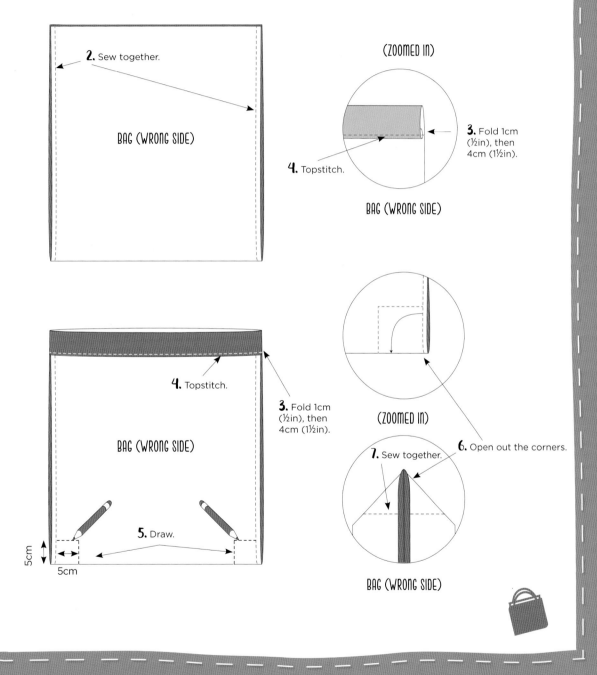

2. Sew together.

BAG (WRONG SIDE)

(ZOOMED IN)

3. Fold 1cm (½in), then 4cm (1½in).

4. Topstitch.

BAG (WRONG SIDE)

4. Topstitch.

3. Fold 1cm (½in), then 4cm (1½in).

BAG (WRONG SIDE)

5. Draw.

5cm

5cm

(ZOOMED IN)

6. Open out the corners.

7. Sew together.

BAG (WRONG SIDE)

Shopping bag
(continued)

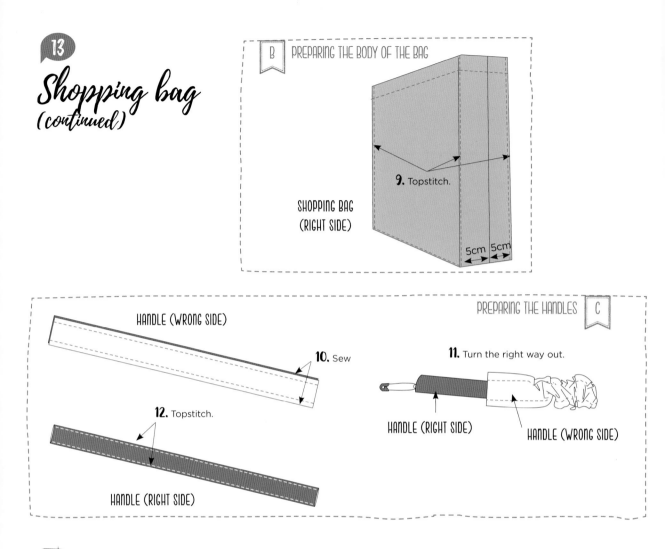

B PREPARING THE BODY OF THE BAG

9. Topstitch.

SHOPPING BAG
(RIGHT SIDE)

5cm 5cm

HANDLE (WRONG SIDE)

10. Sew

12. Topstitch.

HANDLE (RIGHT SIDE)

PREPARING THE HANDLES **C**

11. Turn the right way out.

HANDLE (RIGHT SIDE)

HANDLE (WRONG SIDE)

METHOD (CONTINUED)

8. Turn the bag the right way out.

9. Draw straight vertical lines 5cm (2in) from the side seam of the bag: these will form the edges between the front, back and sides. Fold the fabric along the drawn line and topstitch 2mm (⅛in) from the folded edge, to create a raised ridge for the corners of the bag.

C PREPARING THE HANDLES

10. Pin two of the handle pieces right sides together and sew along the long sides, 1cm (½in) from the edge. Repeat with the two other handle pieces.

11. Turn the handles the right way out, using a safety pin to help.

12. Topstitch the long sides, 2mm (⅛in) from the edge.

D SEWING THE BAG TOGETHER

13. Position the handles on the bag, 11cm (4¼in) from the edges.

14. Fold under 1cm (½in) at each end of the handles and pin and then sew them to the bag, forming a cross shape as shown in the diagram.

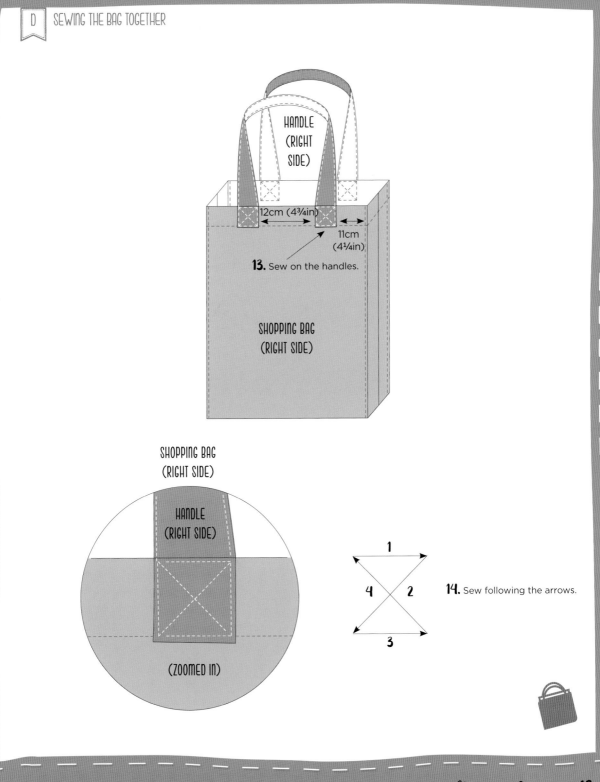

HANDLE
(RIGHT
SIDE)

12cm (4¾in)

11cm
(4¼in)

13. Sew on the handles.

SHOPPING BAG
(RIGHT SIDE)

SHOPPING BAG
(RIGHT SIDE)

HANDLE
(RIGHT SIDE)

(ZOOMED IN)

1

4   2

3

14. Sew following the arrows.

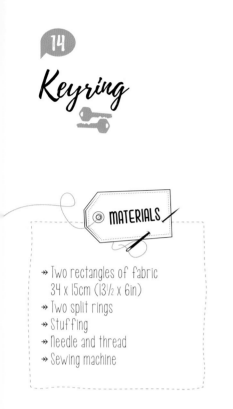

Keyring

14

MATERIALS

→ Two rectangles of fabric
  34 x 15cm (13½ x 6in)
→ Two split rings
→ Stuffing
→ Needle and thread
→ Sewing machine

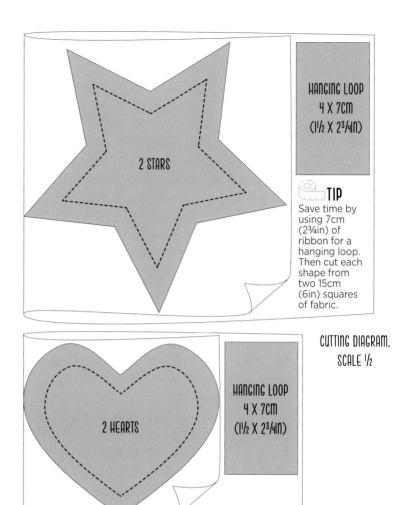

2 STARS

**HANGING LOOP
4 X 7CM
(1½ X 2¾IN)**

TIP

Save time by
using 7cm
(2¾in) of
ribbon for a
hanging loop.
Then cut each
shape from
two 15cm
(6in) squares
of fabric.

2 HEARTS

**HANGING LOOP
4 X 7CM
(1½ X 2¾IN)**

CUTTING DIAGRAM,
SCALE ½

METHOD

A CUTTING

1. Photocopy the shapes above at 200% and cut them out along the unbroken line.

2. Trace the shapes on to the fabric.

3. Cut out the paper shapes along the dotted line.

4. Trace the dotted lines on to the wrong side of the fabric: it will make it easier when you are sewing on the machine.

B SEWING TOGETHER

5. Iron a 1cm (½in) fold along each long side of the hanging loop.

6. Fold in half and topstitch, 2mm (⅛in) from the edge.

7. Fold the hanging loop in half and sew it on to the star or heart.

8. Lay the two pieces of the star or heart right sides together. Sew along the dotted lines, leaving a small opening.

9. Clip the angles and trim down the seam allowances at the tips of the star or the star won't have neat points.

10. Turn the right way out.

11. Fill with stuffing.

12. Sew up the opening by hand. Use slipstitch or ladder stitch for this. Add the split ring to the hanging loop.

5. Iron.

HANGING LOOP (WRONG SIDE)

HANGING LOOP (RIGHT SIDE)

6. Topstitch 2mm (⅛in) from the edge.

7. Sew on the loop.

9. Clip the angles.

8. Sew together.

12. Sew up by hand.

MY FIRST SEWING MACHINE

My CLOTHES & Accessories

15

SKIRT

16

SCARF

★★★

15

Skirt

MATERIALS

→ Cotton fabric 105 x 41cm
  (41¼ x 16¼in) for size 7-8 years
→ Cotton fabric 110 x 47cm
  (43¼ x 18½in) for size 8-9 years
→ Cotton fabric 115 x 53cm
  (45¼ x 20¾in) for size 9-10 years
→ Elastic, 2.5cm (1in) wide and
  length of waist measurement
→ Safety pin
→ Sewing machine

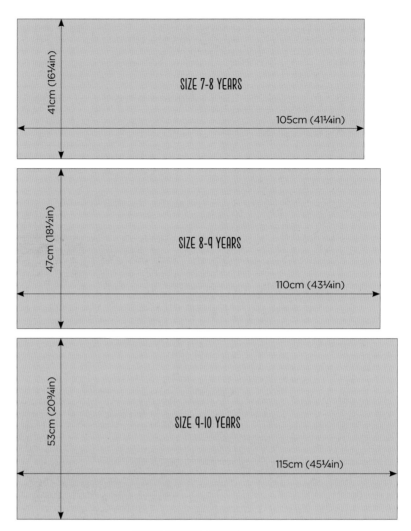

SIZE 7-8 YEARS

41cm (16¼in)

105cm (41¼in)

SIZE 8-9 YEARS

47cm (18½in)

110cm (43¼in)

SIZE 9-10 YEARS

53cm (20¾in)

115cm (45¼in)

CUTTING DIAGRAM, SCALE ⅛

METHOD

A CUTTING

1. Cut a rectangle of fabric according to desired size.

B PREPARING THE SKIRT

2. Fold the fabric in half vertically, right sides together. Sew the short edges of the skirt together, using a 1cm (½in) seam allowance.

3. Make a hem, folding the bottom of the skirt up 1cm (½in) then 2cm (¾in).

4. Topstitch around the top of the hem, 2mm (⅛in) from the edge.

5. Make a hem at the top of the skirt, folding the fabric down 1cm (½in) then 3cm (1¼in). This will be the channel for the elastic.

6. Topstitch the hem 2mm (⅛in) from the fold, leaving an opening of approximately 5cm (2in).

C COMPLETING THE SKIRT

7. Using a safety pin, thread the elastic through the waistband.

8. Overlap the ends of the elastic and sew together.

9. Sew up the opening in the waistband.

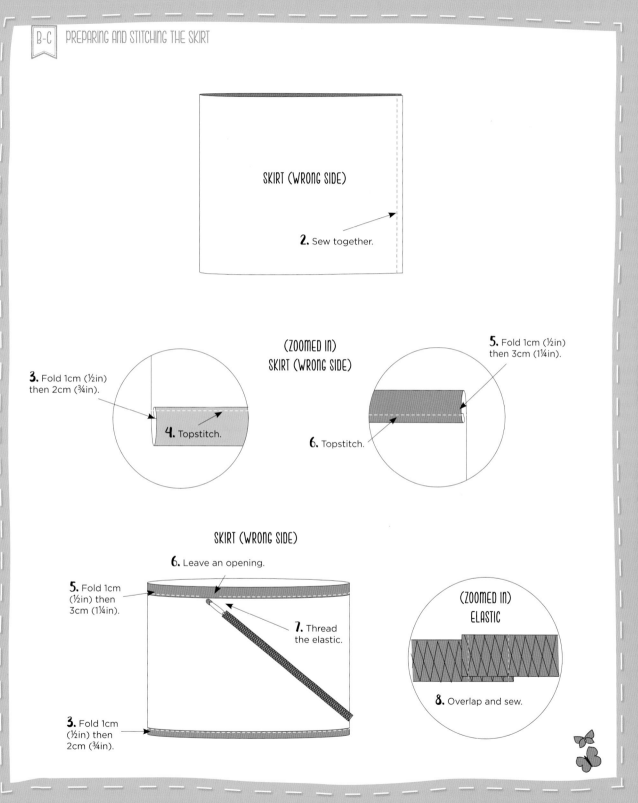

SKIRT (WRONG SIDE)

2. Sew together.

(ZOOMED IN)
SKIRT (WRONG SIDE)

3. Fold 1cm (½in)
then 2cm (¾in).

4. Topstitch.

5. Fold 1cm (½in)
then 3cm (1¼in).

6. Topstitch.

SKIRT (WRONG SIDE)

6. Leave an opening.

5. Fold 1cm
(½in) then
3cm (1¼in).

7. Thread
the elastic.

3. Fold 1cm
(½in) then
2cm (¾in).

(ZOOMED IN)
ELASTIC

8. Overlap and sew.

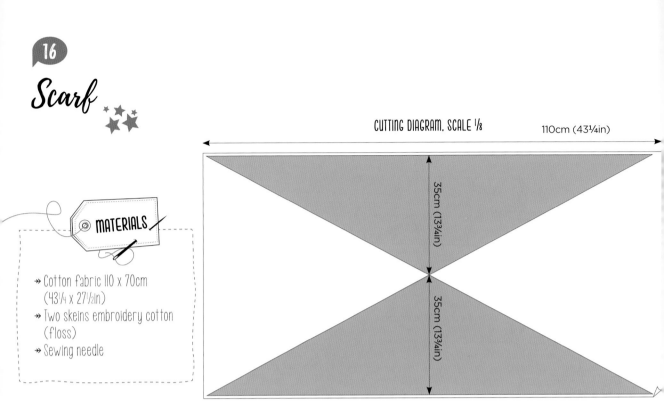

Scarf

16

CUTTING DIAGRAM. SCALE ⅛

110cm (43¼in)

35cm (13¾in)

35cm (13¾in)

MATERIALS

→ Cotton fabric 110 x 70cm
(43¼ x 27½in)
→ Two skeins embroidery cotton
(floss)
→ Sewing needle

METHOD

A CUTTING

1. Cut out two triangles 110cm (43¼in) wide x 35cm (13¾in) high.

B SEWING TOGETHER

2. Pin the triangles right sides together.

3. Sew right round, leaving an opening 5cm (2in) wide and taking a seam allowance of 1cm (½in).

4. Clip the corners (see page 9) and turn the right way out.

C MAKING THE TASSELS

5. Cut 30cm (11¾in) from each skein of cotton.

6. Hold the two skeins together and use one length cut in half to tie a knot round each end.

7. Wrap approximately 10cm (4in) of the other thread round the skeins near each knotted end and tie off.

8. Cut the skeins in half to divide into two tassels.

 TIP
Not sure about making tassels? Buy a pack of ready-made ones online.

D FINISHING TOUCHES

9. Using the remaining thread, hand sew the tassels to the corners of the scarf, passing the needle several times through the loop of the tassel and the point of the scarf.

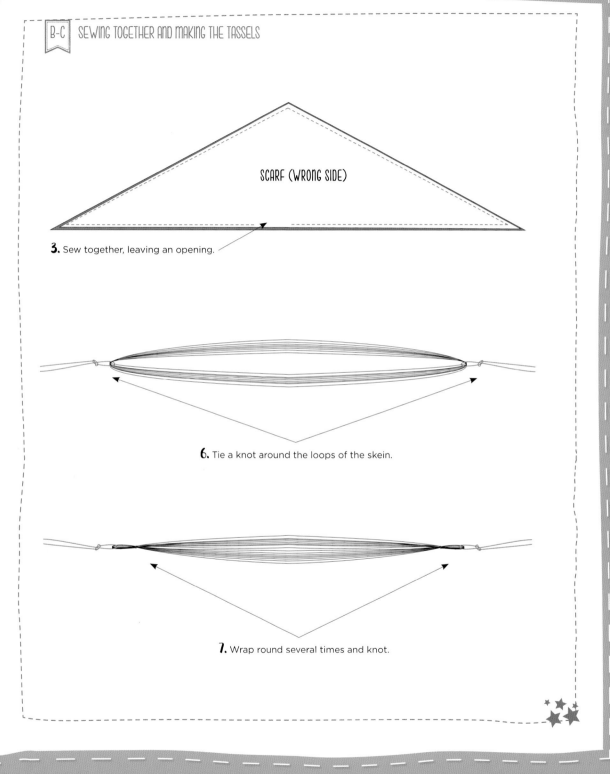

SCARF (WRONG SIDE)

3. Sew together, leaving an opening.

6. Tie a knot around the loops of the skein.

7. Wrap round several times and knot.

17
SCRUNCHIE

18

T-SHIRT REVAMP

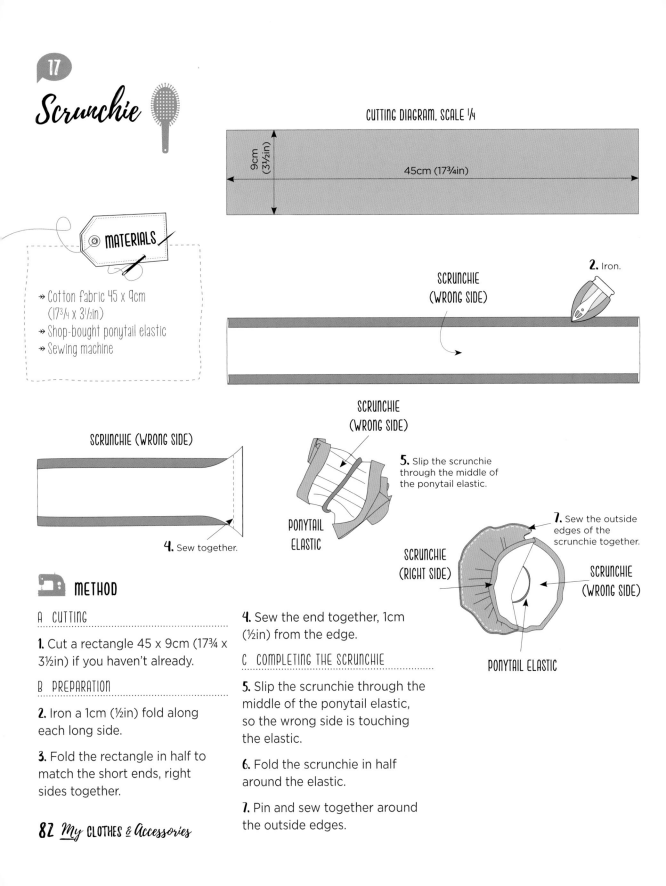

Scrunchie

CUTTING DIAGRAM. SCALE ¼

9cm (3½in)

45cm (17¾in)

MATERIALS

→ Cotton fabric 45 x 9cm (17¾ x 3½in)
→ Shop-bought ponytail elastic
→ Sewing machine

2. Iron.

SCRUNCHIE (WRONG SIDE)

SCRUNCHIE (WRONG SIDE)

5. Slip the scrunchie through the middle of the ponytail elastic.

PONYTAIL ELASTIC

SCRUNCHIE (WRONG SIDE)

4. Sew together.

SCRUNCHIE (RIGHT SIDE)

SCRUNCHIE (WRONG SIDE)

7. Sew the outside edges of the scrunchie together.

PONYTAIL ELASTIC

METHOD

A CUTTING

1. Cut a rectangle 45 x 9cm (17¾ x 3½in) if you haven't already.

B PREPARATION

2. Iron a 1cm (½in) fold along each long side.

3. Fold the rectangle in half to match the short ends, right sides together.

4. Sew the end together, 1cm (½in) from the edge.

C COMPLETING THE SCRUNCHIE

5. Slip the scrunchie through the middle of the ponytail elastic, so the wrong side is touching the elastic.

6. Fold the scrunchie in half around the elastic.

7. Pin and sew together around the outside edges.

18

T-shirt revamp

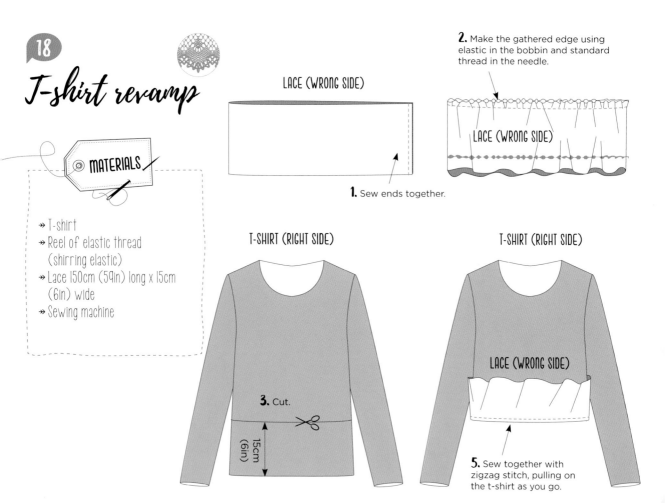

MATERIALS

→ T-shirt
→ Reel of elastic thread (shirring elastic)
→ Lace 150cm (59in) long x 15cm (6in) wide
→ Sewing machine

LACE (WRONG SIDE)

1. Sew ends together.

2. Make the gathered edge using elastic in the bobbin and standard thread in the needle.

LACE (WRONG SIDE)

T-SHIRT (RIGHT SIDE)

3. Cut.

15cm (6in)

T-SHIRT (RIGHT SIDE)

LACE (WRONG SIDE)

5. Sew together with zigzag stitch, pulling on the t-shirt as you go.

METHOD

If your lace has one unfinished edge, or you want a straight appearance, follow the method described. If your lace has two finished edges that you want to make a feature of (as in the photograph) then slip the joined lace over the t-shirt, wrong side of lace to right side of t-shirt, and simply sew around in the same way (using a zigzag stitch and working slowly to keep the gathers evenly distributed).

A PREPARING THE LACE

1. Fold the band of lace right sides facing and sew the ends together, 1cm (½in) from the edge.

2. Gather the top of the lace by winding a bobbin of elastic thread by hand. Insert the bobbin in its case and sew using straight stitch (stitch number 1 on your machine). Don't forget to backstitch at the start and end of the row. The gathers will form automatically.

B SEWING TO THE T-SHIRT

3. Cut 15cm (6in) from the bottom of the t-shirt.

4. Pin the band of lace to the bottom of the t-shirt.

5. Sew the lace to the t-shirt, right sides together, using zigzag stitch and standard thread in the bobbin, working slowly to keep the gathers evenly distributed.

19

NECKLACE

19
Necklace

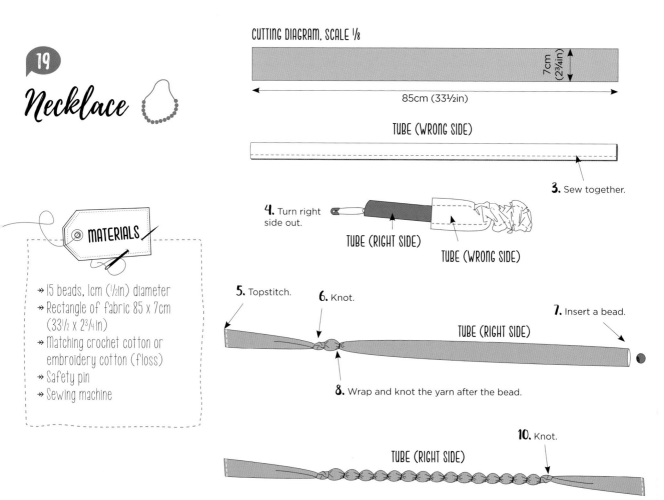

CUTTING DIAGRAM, SCALE ⅛

85cm (33½in)

7cm (2¾in)

TUBE (WRONG SIDE)

3. Sew together.

4. Turn right side out.

TUBE (RIGHT SIDE)

TUBE (WRONG SIDE)

5. Topstitch.

6. Knot.

7. Insert a bead.

TUBE (RIGHT SIDE)

8. Wrap and knot the yarn after the bead.

10. Knot.

TUBE (RIGHT SIDE)

11. Topstitch.

MATERIALS

→ 15 beads, 1cm (½in) diameter
→ Rectangle of fabric 85 x 7cm (33½ x 2¾in)
→ Matching crochet cotton or embroidery cotton (floss)
→ Safety pin
→ Sewing machine

METHOD

A CUTTING

1. Cut a rectangle of fabric 85 x 7cm (33½ x 2¾in) if you haven't already.

B PREPARING THE BAND

2. Fold in half to match the long edges, right sides together.

3. Sew the long edges of the rectangle together, 1cm (½in) from the edge.

4. Turn the fabric tube the right way out, using a safety pin to help.

5. Turn 1cm (½in) inside at one end of the tube and topstitch 2mm (⅛in) from the edge.

6. 15cm (6in) from this end, tie a knot in the tube.

C INSERTING THE BEADS

7. Slip a bead into the open end of the tube.

8. Wrap the cotton/floss several times around the tube just after the bead and tie it in a double knot.

9. Repeat this step with all the beads.

10. After the last bead, tie a knot in the tube.

11. Turn 1cm (½in) from the end inside and topstitch 2mm (⅛in) from the edge.

MY FIRST SEWING MACHINE

FOR My
SATCHEL

20 PENCIL CASE

21

BOOK COVER

20

Pencil case

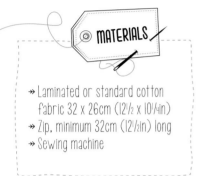

MATERIALS

→ Laminated or standard cotton fabric 32 x 26cm (12½ x 10¼in)
→ Zip, minimum 32cm (12½in) long
→ Sewing machine

CUTTING DIAGRAM, SCALE ⅛

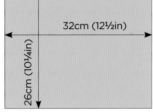

32cm (12½in)

26cm (10¼in)

METHOD

A PUTTING IN THE ZIP

1. Cut a rectangle of fabric 32 x 26cm (12½ x 10¼in) if you haven't already.

2. Pin the zip along one of the longer sides of the pencil case, right sides together.

3. Attach the special zip foot on your sewing machine and adjust the needle position if needed.

4. Sew as close to the teeth of the zip as you can.

5. In the same way, pin and sew the other side of the pencil case to the other side of the zip, right sides together.

B SEWING UP THE SIDES OF THE PENCIL CASE

6. Unzip halfway.

7. Arrange the pencil case, right sides together, positioning the zip in the middle of the rectangle created.

8. Reattach the standard foot to the machine and reset the needle position. Sew up the sides of the pencil case, 1cm (½in) from the edge.

9. Cut off any surplus zip – don't accidentally cut off the zip slider!

10. Draw a 3 x 3cm (1¼ x 1¼in) square at each corner on both sides of the pencil case.

C FORMING THE CORNERS OF THE PENCIL CASE

11. Open out the corners to make box corners by pushing the sewn edge down against the adjacent fold so it makes a point.

12. Sew along the drawn line.

13. Trim the corners to 1cm (½in) from the seam.

14. Turn the pencil case the right way out through the opening in the zip.

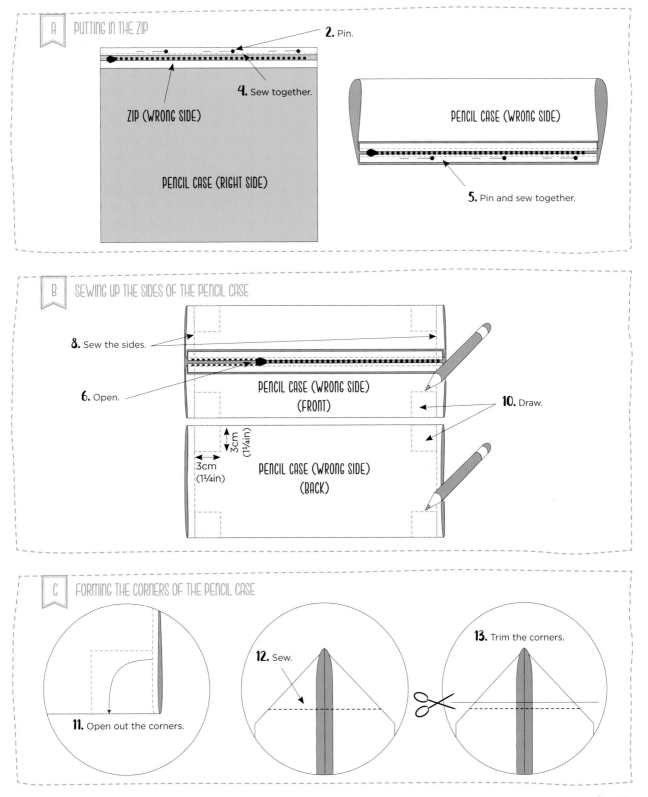

A | PUTTING IN THE ZIP

2. Pin.

4. Sew together.

ZIP (WRONG SIDE)

PENCIL CASE (RIGHT SIDE)

PENCIL CASE (WRONG SIDE)

5. Pin and sew together.

B | SEWING UP THE SIDES OF THE PENCIL CASE

8. Sew the sides.

6. Open.

PENCIL CASE (WRONG SIDE)
(FRONT)

10. Draw.

3cm (1¼in)

3cm (1¼in)

PENCIL CASE (WRONG SIDE)
(BACK)

C | FORMING THE CORNERS OF THE PENCIL CASE

11. Open out the corners.

12. Sew.

13. Trim the corners.

21

Book cover

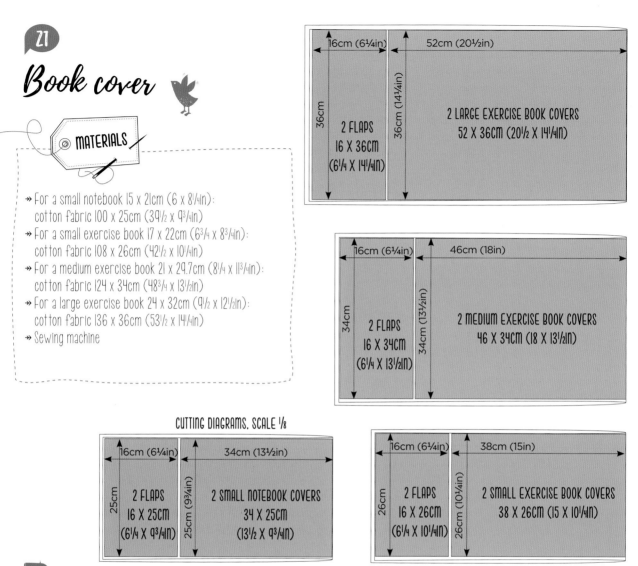

MATERIALS

→ For a small notebook 15 x 21cm (6 x 8¼in):
cotton fabric 100 x 25cm (39½ x 9¾in)

→ For a small exercise book 17 x 22cm (6¾ x 8¾in):
cotton fabric 108 x 26cm (42½ x 10¼in)

→ For a medium exercise book 21 x 29.7cm (8¼ x 11¾in):
cotton fabric 124 x 34cm (48¾ x 13½in)

→ For a large exercise book 24 x 32cm (9½ x 12½in):
cotton fabric 136 x 36cm (53½ x 14¼in)

→ Sewing machine

Diagram labels:

16cm (6¼in) — 52cm (20½in)
36cm — 36cm (14¼in)
2 FLAPS 16 X 36CM (6¼ X 14¼IN)
2 LARGE EXERCISE BOOK COVERS 52 X 36CM (20½ X 14¼IN)

16cm (6¼in) — 46cm (18in)
34cm — 34cm (13½in)
2 FLAPS 16 X 34CM (6¼ X 13½IN)
2 MEDIUM EXERCISE BOOK COVERS 46 X 34CM (18 X 13½IN)

CUTTING DIAGRAMS, SCALE ⅛

16cm (6¼in) — 34cm (13½in)
25cm — 25cm (9¾in)
2 FLAPS 16 X 25CM (6¼ X 9¾IN)
2 SMALL NOTEBOOK COVERS 34 X 25CM (13½ X 9¾IN)

16cm (6¼in) — 38cm (15in)
26cm — 26cm (10¼in)
2 FLAPS 16 X 26CM (6¼ X 10¼IN)
2 SMALL EXERCISE BOOK COVERS 38 X 26CM (15 X 10¼IN)

METHOD

A CUTTING

1. Choose your notebook size, as given above, and cut two cover pieces and two flap pieces to the size stated.

B PREPARING THE FLAPS

1. Fold each flap, wrong sides together, lengthways.

2. Topstitch the long side, stitching within the 1cm (½in) seam allowance.

C SEWING TOGETHER

3. Position and sew the flaps to one book-cover piece, right sides together, using a 1cm (½in) seam allowance.

4. Pin the two book-cover pieces right sides together. Sew all round, leaving a 5cm (2in) opening on one of the long edges.

5. Clip the corners (see page 9).

6. Turn the book cover the right way out through the opening.

7. Topstitch the top and bottom of the book cover, 2mm (⅛in) from the edge.

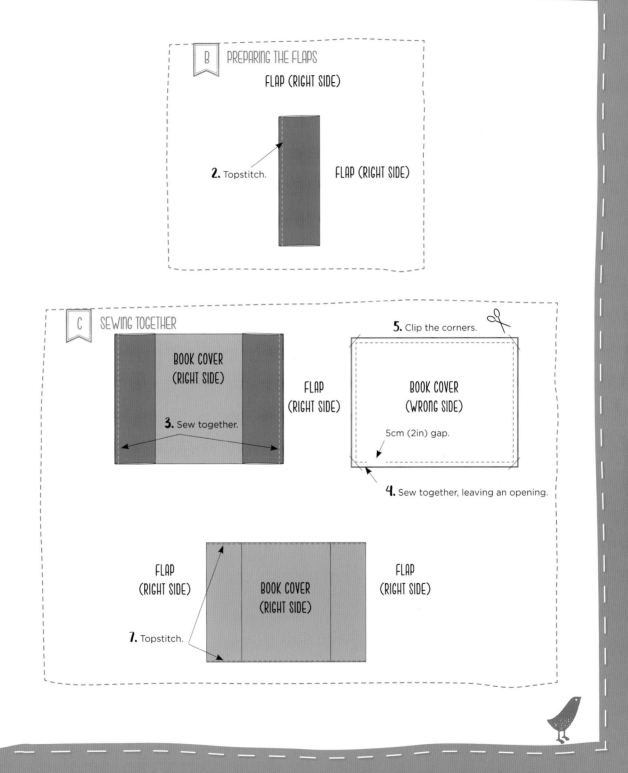

B PREPARING THE FLAPS

FLAP (RIGHT SIDE)

2. Topstitch.

FLAP (RIGHT SIDE)

C SEWING TOGETHER

BOOK COVER
(RIGHT SIDE)

3. Sew together.

FLAP
(RIGHT SIDE)

5. Clip the corners.

BOOK COVER
(WRONG SIDE)

5cm (2in) gap.

4. Sew together, leaving an opening.

FLAP
(RIGHT SIDE)

BOOK COVER
(RIGHT SIDE)

FLAP
(RIGHT SIDE)

7. Topstitch.

ROLL-UP PENCIL CASE

22

23

DRAWSTRING SPORTS BAG

Roll-up pencil case

→ Laminated or standard cotton
   fabric 42 x 64cm (16½ x 25¼in)
→ Button, 22mm (⅞in)
→ Sewing machine

PENCIL COMPARTMENT
38 X 22CM
(15 X 8¾IN)

38cm (15in)

22cm

38cm

21cm

OUTSIDE AND INSIDE OF
CASE 38 X 21CM
(15 X 8¼IN) EACH

38cm

21cm

BUTTON LOOP
4 X 7CM (1½ X 2¾IN)

CUTTING DIAGRAM. SCALE ⅛

METHOD

A CUTTING

1. Cut out:
• One rectangle 38 x 22cm
  (15 x 8¾in)
• Two rectangles 38 x 21cm
  (15 x 8¼in)
• One rectangle 4 x 7cm
  (1½ x 2¾in)

B PENCIL COMPARTMENT

2. Fold the 38 x 22cm (15 x 8¾in)
rectangle, wrong sides together,
so it is 38 x 11cm (15 x 4⅜in).

3. Sew along the bottom, 1cm
(½in) from the edge.

C BUTTON LOOP

4. Iron a 1cm (½in) fold along each
long edge of the button loop.

5. Fold the piece in half and
topstitch, 2mm (⅛in) from
the edge.

6. Fold the button loop as shown
in the diagram.

D SEWING TOGETHER

7. Sew the pencil compartment to
the bottom of the inside case, on
the right side, using a 1cm (½in)
seam allowance.

8. Sew the button loop centrally
to the right edge of the case.

9. Draw vertical lines every 3cm
(1³⁄₁₆in) except at the edges,
where the vertical lines should
be 4cm (1½in) from the edges, as
shown in the diagram.

10. Sew along the vertical lines.

11. Pin and sew the inside and
outside of the case, right sides
together, leaving a 5cm (2in)
opening on the edge opposite
the button loop, using a 1cm
(½in) seam allowance.

12. Clip the corners (see page 9).

13. Turn the pencil case the right
way out through the opening.

14. Topstitch right round the case,
2mm (⅛in) from the edge.

15. Put the pencils in the case,
roll it up and decide where to
position the button.

16. Sew on the button.

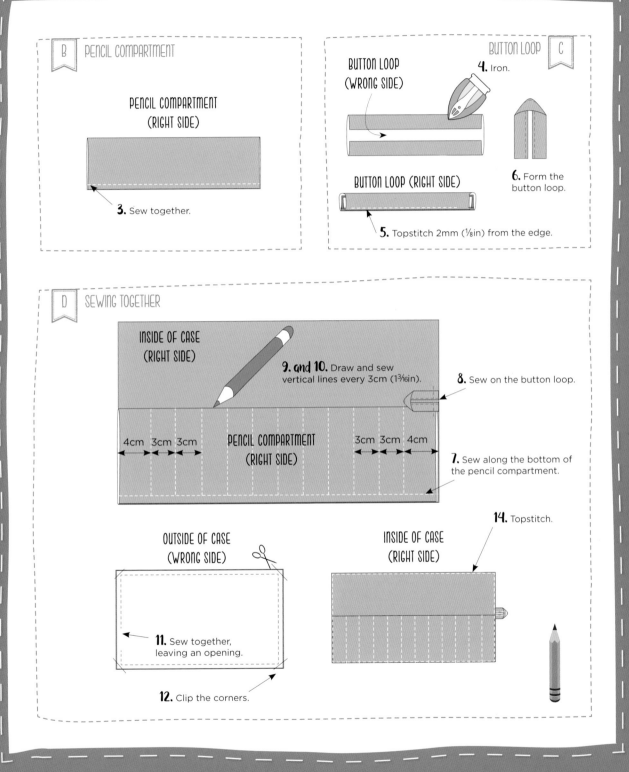

B PENCIL COMPARTMENT

PENCIL COMPARTMENT
(RIGHT SIDE)

3. Sew together.

BUTTON LOOP C

BUTTON LOOP
(WRONG SIDE)

4. Iron.

BUTTON LOOP (RIGHT SIDE)

6. Form the button loop.

5. Topstitch 2mm (⅛in) from the edge.

D SEWING TOGETHER

INSIDE OF CASE
(RIGHT SIDE)

9. and 10. Draw and sew vertical lines every 3cm (1³⁄₁₆in).

8. Sew on the button loop.

4cm 3cm 3cm   PENCIL COMPARTMENT
(RIGHT SIDE)   3cm 3cm 4cm

7. Sew along the bottom of the pencil compartment.

OUTSIDE OF CASE
(WRONG SIDE)

14. Topstitch.

INSIDE OF CASE
(RIGHT SIDE)

11. Sew together, leaving an opening.

12. Clip the corners.

23

Drawstring sports bag

and laundry bag

CUTTING DIAGRAM, SCALE ⅛

70cm

DRAWSTRING
SPORTS BAG
25 X 70CM
(9¾ X 27½IN)

25cm

100cm

LAUNDRY BAG
50 X 100CM (19¾ X 39½IN)

50cm

⊙ MATERIALS

→ Sewing machine
→ Safety pin

For the drawstring sports bag:
→ Cotton fabric 25 x 70cm
  (9¾ x 27½in)
→ Cord 50cm (19¾in)

For the laundry bag:
→ Cotton fabric 50 x 100cm
  (19¾ x 39½in)
→ Cord 100cm (39½in)

 ## METHOD FOR BOTH BAGS

A DRAWSTRING CHANNEL

1. 5cm (2in) from the corner, on each long edge of the bag, make a 1cm (½in) cut, as shown in the diagram.

2. Fold 1cm (½in) to the wrong side of the bag along this 5cm (2in).

3. Topstitch the fold, 2mm (⅛in) from the edge.

4. Form a channel, folding in each short edge of the bag 1cm (½in) then 2cm (¾in).

5. Topstitch the hem, 2mm (⅛in) from the edge.

B SEWING THE SIDES TOGETHER

6. Fold the bag in half, right sides together, matching up the channels.

7. Sew the sides together, 1cm (½in) from the edge.

8. Using a safety pin, thread the cord through the channels and knot the ends together to stop it slipping out.

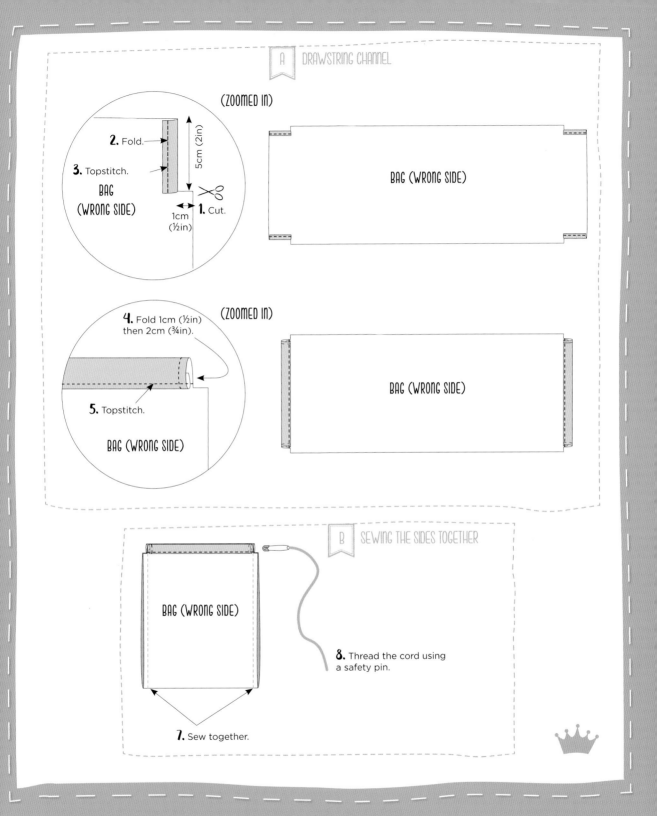

(ZOOMED IN)

2. Fold.

3. Topstitch.

BAG
(WRONG SIDE)

5cm (2in)

1. Cut.

1cm
(½in)

BAG (WRONG SIDE)

(ZOOMED IN)

4. Fold 1cm (½in)
then 2cm (¾in).

5. Topstitch.

BAG (WRONG SIDE)

BAG (WRONG SIDE)

BAG (WRONG SIDE)

8. Thread the cord using
a safety pin.

7. Sew together.

MY FIRST SEWING MACHINE

FOR My
SUITCASE

24

LUGGAGE LABEL

25

BEACH TOWEL

Luggage label

MATERIALS

→ Laminated cotton fabric
  20 x 20cm (8 x 8in)
→ A piece of stiff paper
→ Sewing machine

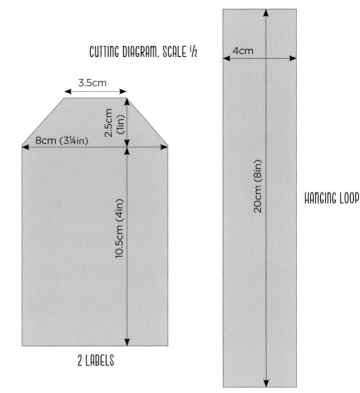

CUTTING DIAGRAM, SCALE ½

3.5cm

2.5cm (1in)

8cm (3¼in)

10.5cm (4in)

2 LABELS

4cm

20cm (8in)

HANGING LOOP

METHOD

A PREPARATION

1. Photocopy the shape above at 200%.

2. Cut the two labels and the hanging loop from laminated cotton fabric.

B MAKING THE HANGING LOOP

3. Make a 1cm (½in) fold along each long side of the hanging loop.

4. Fold the piece in half and topstitch, 2mm (⅛in) from the edge.

5. Fold the hanging loop as shown in the diagram.

6. Sew the hanging loop to one of the label pieces, right sides together, within the 1cm (½in) seam allowance.

C SEWING THE LABEL TOGETHER

7. On the wrong side of the other piece, draw a rectangle, 2.5cm (1in) from each edge.

8. Cut down the middle of the rectangle and into the corners.

9. Fold the flaps back and topstitch 2mm (⅛in) from the edge, round the window created.

10. Pin the two sides of the label right sides facing and sew together, 1cm (½in) from the edge (it is advisable to draw the seam allowance on the wrong side of the label).

11. Clip the corners (see page 9).

12. Turn the label the right way out through the window.

13. Cut a rectangle 6 x 9cm (2½ x 3½in) from the sheet of stiff paper and slip it into the window. Write your name and address on the area of card visible through the window.

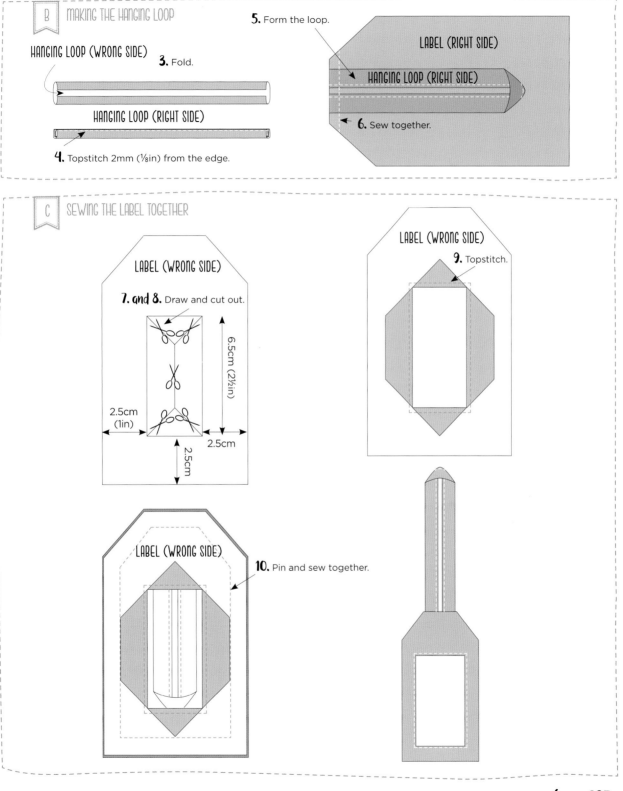

B | MAKING THE HANGING LOOP

HANGING LOOP (WRONG SIDE)

3. Fold.

HANGING LOOP (RIGHT SIDE)

4. Topstitch 2mm (⅛in) from the edge.

5. Form the loop.

LABEL (RIGHT SIDE)

HANGING LOOP (RIGHT SIDE)

6. Sew together.

C | SEWING THE LABEL TOGETHER

LABEL (WRONG SIDE)

7. and 8. Draw and cut out.

6.5cm (2½in)

2.5cm (1in)

2.5cm

2.5cm

LABEL (WRONG SIDE)

9. Topstitch.

LABEL (WRONG SIDE)

10. Pin and sew together.

25

Beach towel

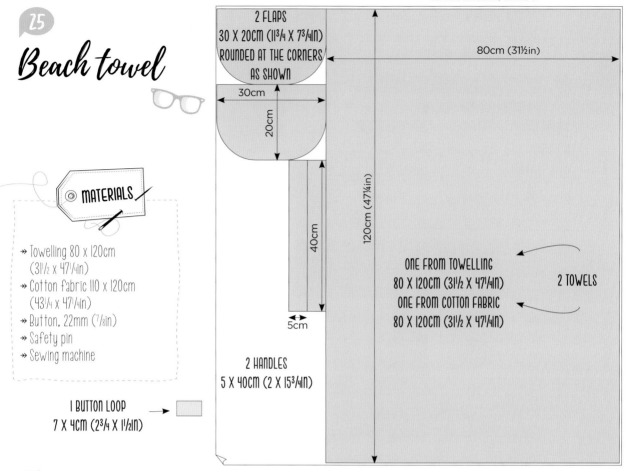

2 FLAPS
30 X 20CM (11³/₄ X 7³/₄IN)
ROUNDED AT THE CORNERS
AS SHOWN

30cm

20cm

80cm (31½in)

120cm (47¼in)

40cm

5cm

ONE FROM TOWELLING
80 X 120CM (31½ X 47¼IN)
ONE FROM COTTON FABRIC
80 X 120CM (31½ X 47¼IN)

2 TOWELS

2 HANDLES
5 X 40CM (2 X 15³/₄IN)

⊙ MATERIALS

→ Towelling 80 x 120cm
  (31½ x 47¼in)
→ Cotton fabric 110 x 120cm
  (43¼ x 47¼in)
→ Button, 22mm (⁷/₈in)
→ Safety pin
→ Sewing machine

I BUTTON LOOP
7 X 4CM (2³/₄ X 1½IN)

🪡 METHOD

A CUTTING

1. From towelling cut one rectangle 80 x 120cm (31½ x 47¼in) if you haven't already
From cotton cut:
• One rectangle 80 x 120cm (31½ x 47¼in)
• Two rectangles 5 x 40cm (2 x 15¾in)
• Two rectangles with rounded corners, as shown in the diagram, 30 x 20cm (11¾ x 7¾in)
• One rectangle 7 x 4cm (2¾ x 1½in)

B MAKING THE BUTTON LOOP

2. Iron a 1cm (½in) fold along each long edge of the small rectangle.

3. Fold it in half and topstitch, 2mm (⅛in) from the edge.

4. Fold the button loop as shown in the diagram.

C SEWING THE FLAP

5. Sew on the button loop, right sides together, in the middle of one of the flaps, within the 1cm (½in) seam allowance.

6. Pin the two flap pieces right sides together, then sew around the rounded edge.

7. Turn the right way out.

8. Topstitch around the curve, 2mm (⅛in) from the edge.

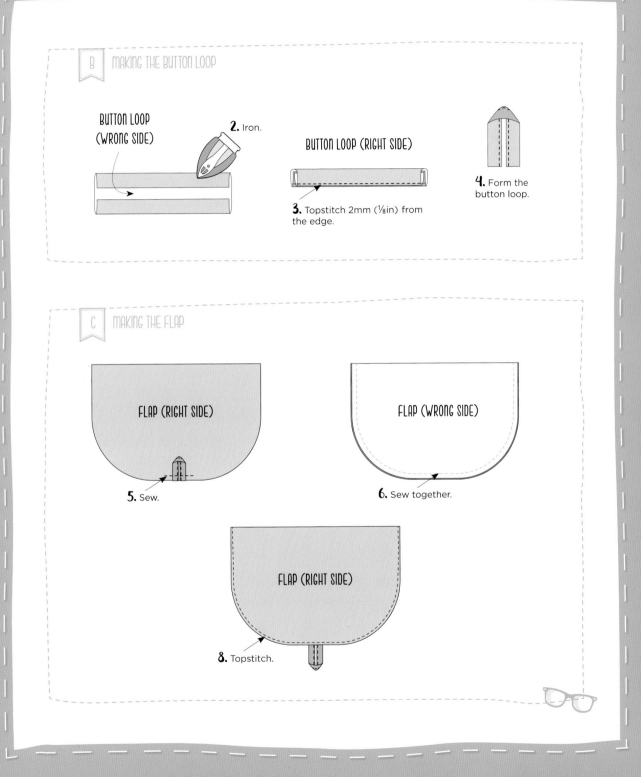

BUTTON LOOP
(WRONG SIDE)

2. Iron.

BUTTON LOOP (RIGHT SIDE)

3. Topstitch 2mm (⅛in) from the edge.

4. Form the button loop.

C | MAKING THE FLAP

FLAP (RIGHT SIDE)

5. Sew.

FLAP (WRONG SIDE)

6. Sew together.

FLAP (RIGHT SIDE)

8. Topstitch.

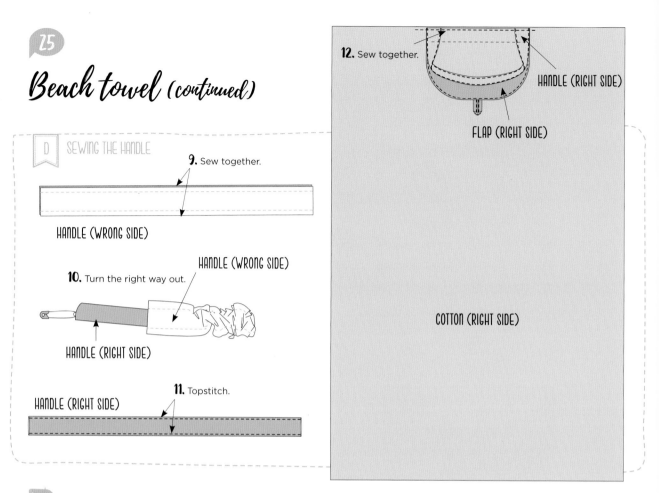

Beach towel (continued)

D SEWING THE HANDLE

9. Sew together.

HANDLE (WRONG SIDE)

HANDLE (WRONG SIDE)

10. Turn the right way out.

HANDLE (RIGHT SIDE)

HANDLE (RIGHT SIDE)

11. Topstitch.

12. Sew together.

HANDLE (RIGHT SIDE)

FLAP (RIGHT SIDE)

COTTON (RIGHT SIDE)

METHOD (CONTINUED)

D SEWING THE HANDLE

9. Sew the long edges of the handle together, 1cm (½in) from the edge, right sides facing.

10. Turn the handle the right way out, using a safety pin to help.

11. Topstitch the long sides, 2mm (⅛in) from the edge.

12. Place the flap in the middle of the short side of the cotton piece, right sides together. Position the handle under the flap, then sew through all layers, within the 1cm (½in) seam allowance.

E COMPLETING THE TOWEL

13. Lay the cotton and towelling rectangles right sides together then sew all round, taking a 1cm (½in) seam allowance and leaving a 10cm (4in) gap in one side.

14. Turn the right way out and topstitch right round the towel.

15. Fold the towel in three, lengthways, then roll it up.

16. Sew on a button to align with the button loop.

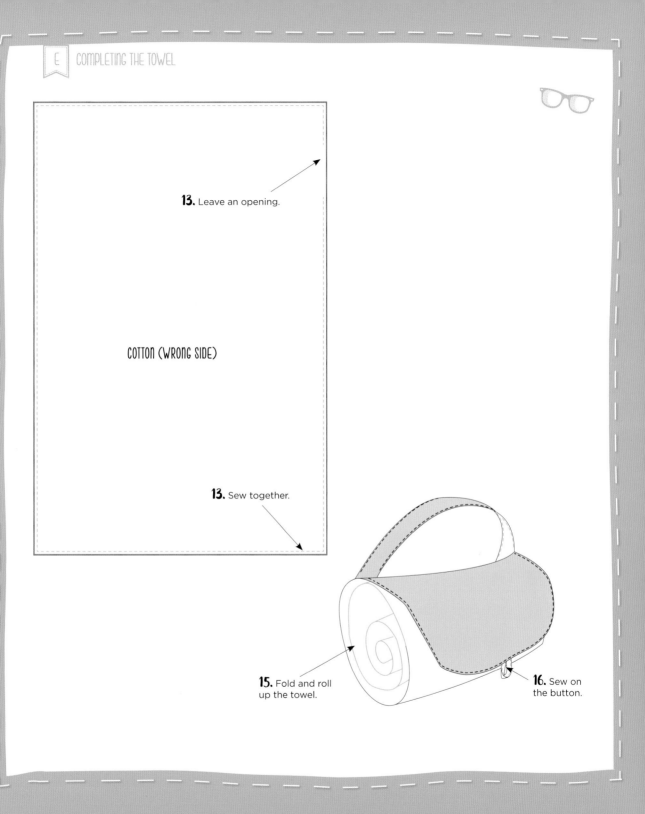

13. Leave an opening.

COTTON (WRONG SIDE)

13. Sew together.

15. Fold and roll up the towel.

16. Sew on the button.

HAIR-CLIP CASE

27

HEADBAND

26

Hair-clip case

25cm (9¾in)

20cm (7¾in)

2 RECTANGLES

⊚ MATERIALS

→ Fabric 50 x 20cm (19¾ x 7¾in)
→ 130cm (51¼in) grosgrain ribbon, 2cm (¾in) wide
→ Sewing machine

METHOD

A CUTTING

1. Cut two rectangles of fabric 25 x 20cm (9¾ x 7¾in).

B PREPARING THE INSIDE

2. Attach two 25cm (9¾in) lengths of grosgrain ribbon lengthways along the right side of the rectangle that will be the inside of the case, approximately 5cm (2in) from the edge. Sew within the 1cm (½in) seam allowance.

3. Sew across the ribbon one-third and two-thirds of the way along.

C PREPARING THE OUTSIDE

4. Attach the centre of the remaining ribbon in the middle of the outside rectangle of the case, on the right side. Temporarily knot the ends of the ribbon together so they don't get caught in the next seam.

D COMPLETING THE CASE

5. Lay the two rectangles right sides together.

6. Sew right round, 1cm (½in) from the edge, leaving an opening of approximately 7cm (2¾in) so you can turn it the right way out.

7. Clip the corners then turn the case the right way out (see page 9).

8. Topstitch right round the rectangle, 2mm (⅛in) from the edge.

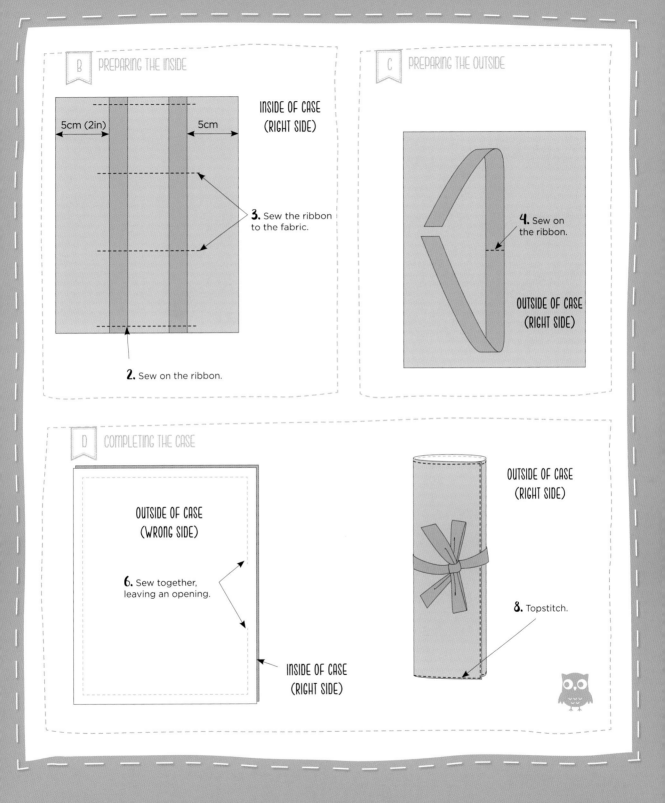

B PREPARING THE INSIDE

INSIDE OF CASE
(RIGHT SIDE)

5cm (2in) 5cm

3. Sew the ribbon to the fabric.

2. Sew on the ribbon.

C PREPARING THE OUTSIDE

4. Sew on the ribbon.

OUTSIDE OF CASE
(RIGHT SIDE)

D COMPLETING THE CASE

OUTSIDE OF CASE
(WRONG SIDE)

6. Sew together, leaving an opening.

INSIDE OF CASE
(RIGHT SIDE)

OUTSIDE OF CASE
(RIGHT SIDE)

8. Topstitch.

27

Headband

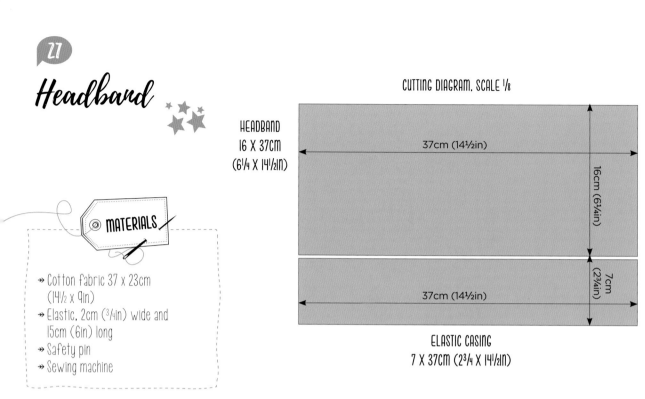

CUTTING DIAGRAM. SCALE ⅛

HEADBAND
16 X 37CM
(6¼ X 14½IN)

37cm (14½in)

16cm (6¼in)

7cm (2¾in)

37cm (14½in)

ELASTIC CASING
7 X 37CM (2¾ X 14½IN)

MATERIALS

→ Cotton fabric 37 x 23cm
  (14½ x 9in)
→ Elastic, 2cm (¾in) wide and
  15cm (6in) long
→ Safety pin
→ Sewing machine

METHOD

A CUTTING

1. Cut one headband piece and one elastic casing piece to the sizes given in the diagram above.

B PREPARING THE WIDE BAND

2. Iron a double 1cm (½in) fold along each long edge of the headband.

3. Topstitch 2mm (⅛in) from the edge.

C PREPARING THE ELASTIC CASING

4. Fold the elastic casing in half lengthways, right sides together and sew down its length, 1cm (½in) from the edge.

5. Turn the band the right way out, using a safety pin to help.

6. Thread the elastic through the casing, using a safety pin.

7. Hold the elastic in place at both ends of the casing with a few stitches.

D SEWING TOGETHER

8. Fold the headband, right sides together. Sew for 3cm (1¼in), 3cm (1¼in) from the fold.

9. Open out and press flat.

10. Position the elasticated piece on the end you have just folded out, right sides together.

11. Bring the long sides of the headband over the elasticated piece so it is now sandwiched in the middle of the main headband piece.

12. Sew together 1cm (½in) from the end.

13. Repeat steps 9–11 at the other end of the headband.

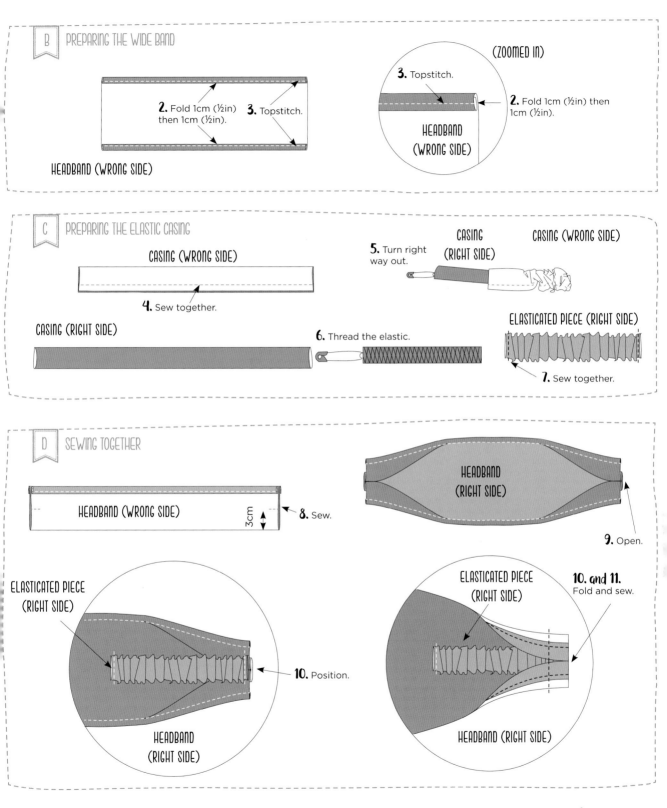

B — PREPARING THE WIDE BAND

2. Fold 1cm (½in) then 1cm (½in).

3. Topstitch.

HEADBAND (WRONG SIDE)

(ZOOMED IN)

3. Topstitch.

2. Fold 1cm (½in) then 1cm (½in).

HEADBAND (WRONG SIDE)

C — PREPARING THE ELASTIC CASING

CASING (WRONG SIDE)

4. Sew together.

CASING (RIGHT SIDE)

5. Turn right way out.

CASING (RIGHT SIDE)

CASING (WRONG SIDE)

6. Thread the elastic.

ELASTICATED PIECE (RIGHT SIDE)

7. Sew together.

D — SEWING TOGETHER

HEADBAND (WRONG SIDE)

3cm

8. Sew.

HEADBAND (RIGHT SIDE)

9. Open.

ELASTICATED PIECE (RIGHT SIDE)

10. Position.

HEADBAND (RIGHT SIDE)

ELASTICATED PIECE (RIGHT SIDE)

10. and 11. Fold and sew.

HEADBAND (RIGHT SIDE)

MY FIRST SEWING MACHINE

For the
KITCHEN

28

APRON

29

OVEN GLOVE

Apron

MATERIALS

→ Cotton fabric 100 x 60cm (39½ x 23¾in)
→ 2m (78¾in) ribbon, 2cm (¾in) wide
→ Safety pin
→ Sewing machine

CUTTING DIAGRAM. SCALE ⅛

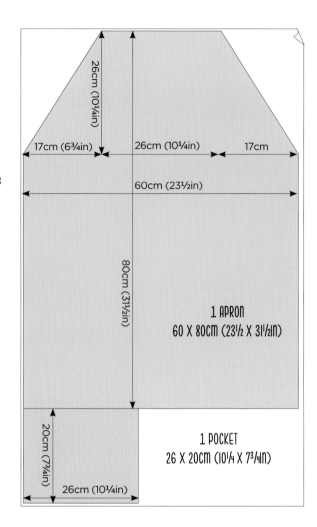

26cm (10¼in)

17cm (6¾in)   26cm (10¼in)   17cm

60cm (23½in)

80cm (31½in)

1 APRON
60 X 80CM (23½ X 31½IN)

20cm (7¾in)

26cm (10¼in)

1 POCKET
26 X 20CM (10¼ X 7¾IN)

METHOD

A CUTTING

1. Cut a rectangle 26 x 20cm (10¼ x 7¾in) for the pocket. Cut a 60 x 80cm (23½ x 31½in) rectangle, and trim it as shown in the diagram above.

B HEMMING

2. Hem the apron by folding over 1cm (½in) then 2cm (¾in) at the top, the sides and then the bottom.

3. Topstitch the hems, 2mm (⅛in) from the edge.

4. On the diagonals, fold over 1cm (½in) then 3cm (1¼in) to form a casing and topstitch.

5. Turn in 1cm (½in) along the sides of the pocket and topstitch.

6. Hem the top of the pocket: fold over 1cm (½in) then 2cm (¾in) and topstitch.

C COMPLETING THE APRON

7. Position the pocket on the apron as shown, right sides together, 15cm (6in) from the edges of the apron and 20cm (7¾in) from the bottom of the diagonal edges.

8. Sew on the bottom of the pocket, 1cm (½in) from the edge.

9. Fold the pocket upwards and sew up the sides of the pocket.

10. Using a safety pin, thread the ribbon through the casings of the diagonal edges.

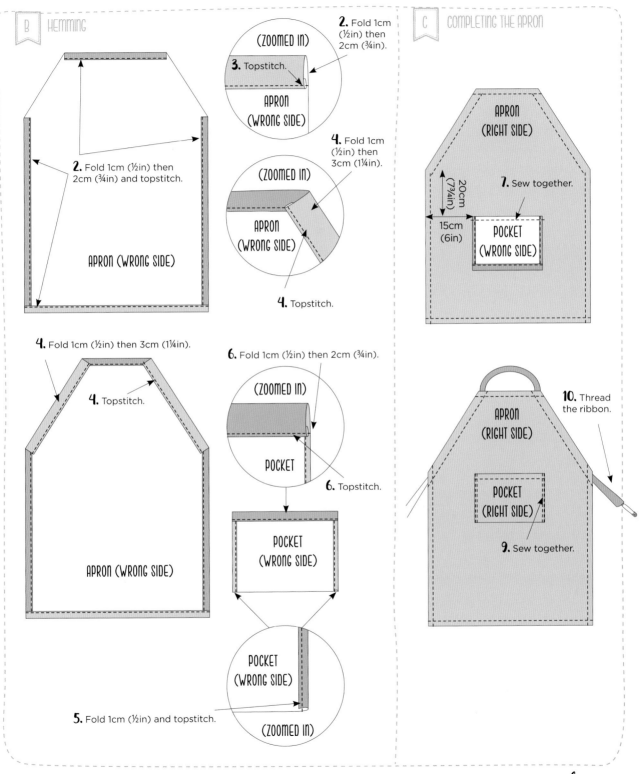

2. Fold 1cm (½in) then 2cm (¾in) and topstitch.

APRON (WRONG SIDE)

2. Fold 1cm (½in) then 2cm (¾in).

(ZOOMED IN)

3. Topstitch.

APRON (WRONG SIDE)

4. Fold 1cm (½in) then 3cm (1¼in).

(ZOOMED IN)

APRON (WRONG SIDE)

4. Topstitch.

4. Fold 1cm (½in) then 3cm (1¼in).

4. Topstitch.

APRON (WRONG SIDE)

6. Fold 1cm (½in) then 2cm (¾in).

(ZOOMED IN)

POCKET

6. Topstitch.

POCKET (WRONG SIDE)

POCKET (WRONG SIDE)

5. Fold 1cm (½in) and topstitch.

(ZOOMED IN)

APRON (RIGHT SIDE)

20cm (7¾in)

15cm (6in)

7. Sew together.

POCKET (WRONG SIDE)

APRON (RIGHT SIDE)

10. Thread the ribbon.

POCKET (RIGHT SIDE)

9. Sew together.

29
Oven glove

⊙ MATERIALS

→ Quilted cotton fabric 82 x 31cm
(32¼ x 12¼in)
→ Sewing machine

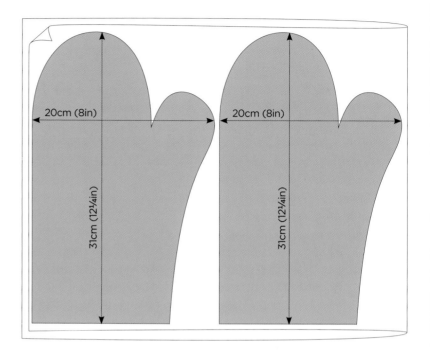

20cm (8in)   20cm (8in)

31cm (12¼in)   31cm (12¼in)

CUTTING DIAGRAM, SCALE ¼

METHOD

A PREPARATION

1. Photocopy the glove shape at 400%.

2. Cut out the paper glove.

3. Cut out four fabric gloves using the paper template, cutting from folded fabric so that you get two symmetrical pairs (see the cutting diagram).

B SEWING TOGETHER

4. Lay the gloves together in pairs, right sides together, then sew round 1cm (½in) from the edge.

5. Trim round the curves 5mm (¼in) from the seam.

6. Clip right to the seam in the angle between the thumb and the finger section.

7. Turn one of the gloves the right way out and slip it inside the other glove.

8. Sew round the base of the glove, leaving an opening of approximately 7cm (2¾in) so you can turn it the right way out.

9. Turn the glove the right way out and topstitch 2mm (⅛in) round the base of the glove.

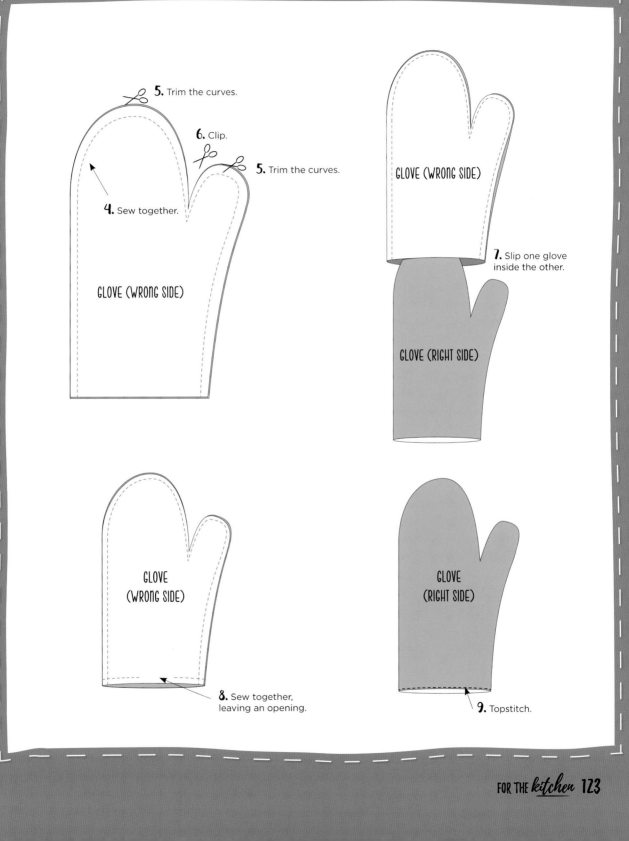

5. Trim the curves.

6. Clip.

5. Trim the curves.

4. Sew together.

GLOVE (WRONG SIDE)

GLOVE (WRONG SIDE)

7. Slip one glove inside the other.

GLOVE (RIGHT SIDE)

GLOVE (WRONG SIDE)

GLOVE (RIGHT SIDE)

8. Sew together, leaving an opening.

9. Topstitch.

30

CAKE BAG

30
Cake bag

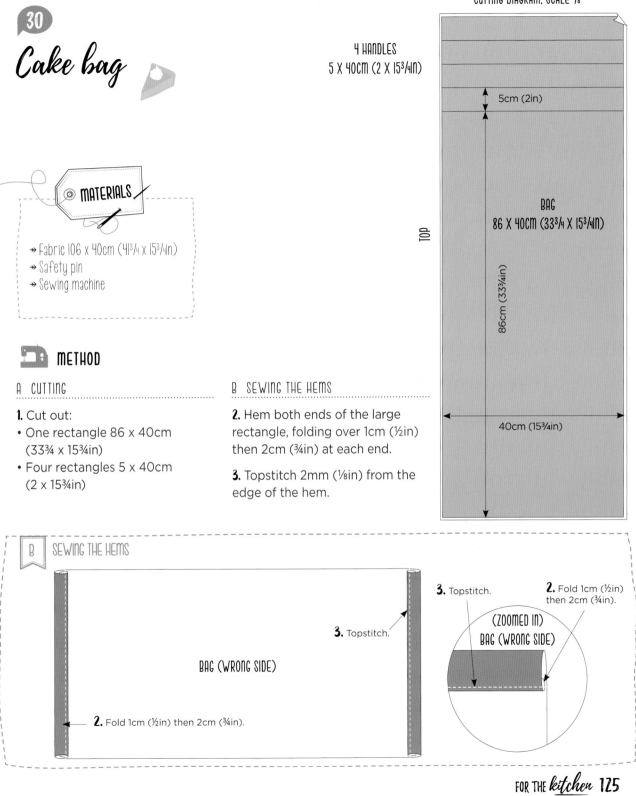

MATERIALS

→ Fabric 106 x 40cm (41¾ x 15¾in)
→ Safety pin
→ Sewing machine

METHOD

A CUTTING

1. Cut out:
• One rectangle 86 x 40cm (33¾ x 15¾in)
• Four rectangles 5 x 40cm (2 x 15¾in)

B SEWING THE HEMS

2. Hem both ends of the large rectangle, folding over 1cm (½in) then 2cm (¾in) at each end.

3. Topstitch 2mm (⅛in) from the edge of the hem.

CUTTING DIAGRAM, SCALE ⅛

4 HANDLES
5 X 40CM (2 X 15¾IN)

TOP

5cm (2in)

BAG
86 X 40CM (33¾ X 15¾IN)

86cm (33¾in)

40cm (15¾in)

B SEWING THE HEMS

BAG (WRONG SIDE)

3. Topstitch.

2. Fold 1cm (½in) then 2cm (¾in).

3. Topstitch.

2. Fold 1cm (½in) then 2cm (¾in).

(ZOOMED IN)
BAG (WRONG SIDE)

Cake bag
(continued)

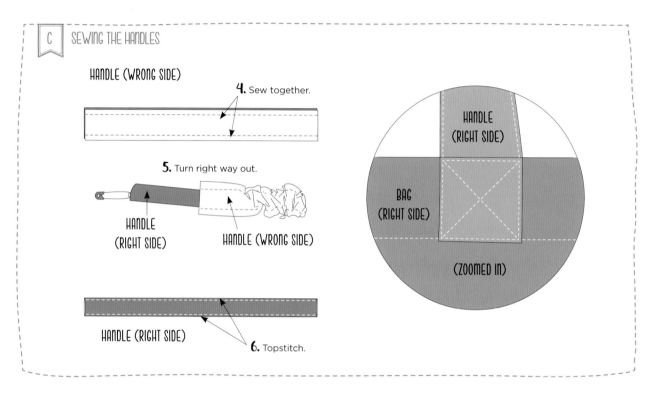

C | SEWING THE HANDLES

HANDLE (WRONG SIDE)

4. Sew together.

5. Turn right way out.

HANDLE (RIGHT SIDE)

HANDLE (WRONG SIDE)

HANDLE (RIGHT SIDE)

6. Topstitch.

HANDLE (RIGHT SIDE)

BAG (RIGHT SIDE)

(ZOOMED IN)

METHOD (CONTINUED)

C SEWING THE HANDLES

4. Pin two of the handle pieces right sides together, and sew along the long sides 1cm (½in) from the edge. Repeat with the two other handle pieces.

5. Turn the handles the right way out, using a safety pin to help.

6. Topstitch the long sides, 2mm (⅛in) from the edge.

7. Pin the handles 11cm (4¼in) from the edges of the bag below the hem.

8. Fold under 1cm (½in) at each end of the handles.

9. Sew them to the bag, forming a cross shape as shown in the diagrams.

D SEWING TOGETHER

10. Fold the short edges of the bag to the middle and sew along each side.

11. Turn the bag the right way out and you're finished.

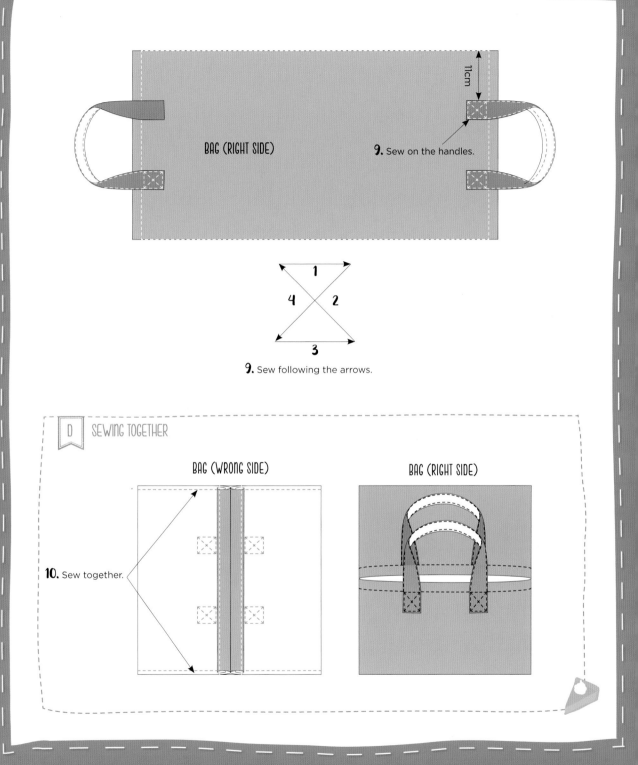

BAG (RIGHT SIDE)

11cm

9. Sew on the handles.

1
4   2
3

9. Sew following the arrows.

SEWING TOGETHER

BAG (WRONG SIDE)

BAG (RIGHT SIDE)

10. Sew together.

ACKNOWLEDGEMENTS

Thanks to Linna Morata and France Duval Stalla for their beautiful fabrics.

France Duval-Stalla

First published in Great Britain 2024 by
Search Press Limited
Wellwood, North Farm Road,
Tunbridge Wells, Kent TN2 3DR

Original title: *Atelier machine à coudre enfants* © 2016,
Éditions Marie Claire – Société d'Information et Créations – SIC

English translation by Burravoe Translation Services

French edition:
Director of publishing: Thierry Lamarre
Publisher: Adeline Lobut
Production and text: Coralie Bijasson
Photographs: Jean-Baptiste Pellerin
Styling: Dominique Turbé
Editing/proofreading: Isabelle Misery
Page-setting and cover: Either Studio
Background and illustrations: Freepik; Damien Payet

ISBN: 978-1-80092-158-0
ebook ISBN: 978-1-80093-146-6

Suppliers
If you have difficulty in obtaining any of the materials and
equipment mentioned in this book, then please visit the Search
Press website for details of suppliers:
www.searchpress.com

Bookmarked Hub
For further ideas and inspiration, and to join our free online
community, visit www.bookmarkedhub.com

The projects in this book have been made using metric
measurements, and the imperial equivalents provided have been
calculated following standard conversion practices. The imperial
measurements are often rounded to the nearest $\frac{1}{8}$in for ease
of use except in rare circumstances; however, if you need more
exact measurements, there are a number of excellent online
converters that you can use. Always use either metric or imperial
measurements, not a combination of both.